## Advance Praise for *My Beloved and My Friend*

**Annie Kate Aarnoutse** at **Tea Time with Annie Kate**: *"My Beloved and My Friend* ... is **a refreshing change from standard marriage books.** No psychobabble. Honest and transparent stories from a couple that has been married for 26 years and friends for even longer. Cheerful but realistic encouragement. And, above all, careful Biblical explanations."

**Mrs. White** at **Legacy of Home**: "The tone of the book is open, friendly, conversational—mixed with some powerful lessons, and incredible insight."

**Steve Blackston** at **Husband of a Homeschool Mom**: "Nothing is held back as they use God's word to show a clear path to being a Godly couple and having a marriage that shows it as well."

**Phyllis Sather**, author of *Purposeful Planning*: "Hal and Melanie have a way of writing that makes you feel as though you are sitting down and having a conversation with them. What they write is solid. What they write is Biblical. What they write actually works and is doable. They don't pull punches or just try to make you feel good. They handle delicate issues with Biblical responses. Since we know that God's word never returns void, we know that this book will change lives."

**Debra Brinkman** at **Footprints in the Butter**: "Hal and Melanie Young have written another fabulous and much-needed book ... [a] brilliant book. Of course it is; I knew it would be."

**Danielle Foltz** at **Raising Little Rhodies**: "Hal & Melanie's book left me hungering more for Jesus and wanting to have a deeper relationship with my spouse. We were friends first but sometimes in the guts of life it's easy to lose sight of that. To get caught up in the surviving. I love that Hal & Melanie are reminding couples like us that love is an action."

**Laurie Bostwick** at **Our Abundant Blessings**: "**This book felt more like a conversation with friends than a how-to manual.** This is not a "rekindle your romance" kind of book. It's also not a "here's why you fight, now work around it" kind of book. It's a straightforward story of how two sinners, saved by Grace, live out their marriage convenant while being best friends. **It's the perfect kind of marriage book.**

**Pastor Dave Buller** at **Christian First**: "Faith should impact your behavior. This one truth, emphasized repeatedly in the Bible, prompts Jesus' followers to adopt Jesus' priorities and Jesus' behaviors in our human relationships. In this book, Hal and Melanie seize this understanding and seek to apply it to the covenant relationship of marriage."

**Kimberly Huff** at **Natural Beach Living**: "This book was hard to put down, I have pages dog eared, I have highlighted sections that I want to return to and I've shared several great passages with my husband. I love how Hal and Melanie Young shared their private life and the struggles that they have gone through. I felt like I was a special friend that they were confiding in and in return I was learning so much about myself."

**Miranda Hupp** at **The Pebble Pond**: "I walked away from this book feeling revived. It is so easy to just live. To just go about the day to day and forget how wonderful being best friends with your husband can actually be! I loved that Hal and Melanie gave real life examples. I also loved that they did not shy away from controversial topics."

**Crystal Blomgren** at **Created for Home**: *"My Beloved and My Friend* is a book that will help spur you to look for the good in your spouse, plant hope to seed into your marriage, and give you the tools to buck the trends of our society."

**Erin** at **Water on the Floor**: "If you have a group of couples to get together, this book would make **such** a fantastic book study. You will **all** be blessed by reading it and together figuring out how you can apply the principles they discuss in your own lives...I'm telling you...this book is **wonderful!**"

**Isabelle Lussier** at **Canadianladybug Reviews**: "The book is a jewel in itself because I find that many marriages would need to read the words included in this book.   Actually, I seriously think that engaged couples should read it together in order to start on the right foot on their walk together."

**Leah Mastilock** at **Sandy Toes Creations**: "The answers are from scripture and explained in a way anyone can understand and apply them. And written by people who understand! Who have lived through some of the worst storms and are still holding strong to each other."

**From an early reviewer**: "After reading this wonderful marriage "toolbox" together with my Dear Hubby we can see that we don't lack "Love", we lack "Friendship". We have lost touch of one another.  Instead of keeping our heads down and doing the Daily Life thing, we need to carve out our time. We need to go back 16 years where it all started and rekindle the friendship we once had. Has it worked? I say it has and he will agree with me."

**Sarah Avila** at **My Joy-Filled Life**: "If you want a Christ-centered, Bible-based guide to marriage, this is it!"

# MY BELOVED AND MY FRIEND

# My Beloved and My Friend

How To Be Married To Your Best Friend
Without Changing Spouses

## Hal and Melanie Young

**Great Waters Press**
Making Biblical Family Life Practical

# My Beloved and My Friend

## Publisher's Cataloging-in-Publication Data

Young, Hal, 1964.
My beloved and my friend: how to be married to your best friend without changing spouses/ Hal and Melanie Young
268p. ; 23cm.
ISBN-10: 1-938554-03-5 (pbk)
ISBN-13: 978-1-938554-03-2 (pbk)
I.Marriage—Religious Aspects—Christianity I.Young, Melanie II. Title
BV835.Y68 2013
248.8
Library of Congress Control Number: 2013942821

# Contents

# Dedication

*To our parents*
*Bill and Brenda Smith*
*and*
*Harral and Norma Young*

*Who gave us a vision and an example*
*of what marriage and friendship*
*can and should be*

# Introduction

*This is my beloved, and this is my friend.*
— Song of Solomon 5:16

Anyone who thinks the Bible is boring obviously never encountered the Song of Solomon. A dozen pages or so, wedged between the existential crisis of Ecclesiastes and the awestruck prophecies of Isaiah, is a piece of romantic poetry so descriptive that rabbis used to recommend young men put it aside until they were thirty. It's one of the few passages we'd suggest *not* reading in church.

We *do* recommend reading it if you're married, or about to be. It has a lot to say about the sheer joy of marital love, whatever aspect is in view—emotional, spiritual, physical, or any other. And in the middle of the rapturous dialogue between the bride and bridegroom, there is this one observation: *This is my beloved, and this is my friend.*

As it happens, the bride delivers this line, but if the Puritan commentators were right, the passage may also be God's people expressing love for their Savior. There's nothing uniquely feminine about that. Shouldn't we look at our spouse and see not only our lover, but our friend?

Somewhere we've lost sight of that, culturally.

We met at college, both of us on scholarship and living in a dormitory converted from the campus hotel. We had become friends, nothing more in mind at the time, when Melanie's mother paid a visit one weekend. The three of us chanced to meet in front of the elevators, so Melanie introduced Hal to her mom. Pleasantries were exchanged, the elevator arrived, and the two ladies boarded. The doors closed.

"That's the man you're going to marry," her mother said, completely out of the blue.

"No way," Melanie shot back. "He's a *friend.*" *And I don't want to mess that up,* she thought to herself.

To our surprise, Melanie's mom was right. Less than three years later, we were engaged, and the summer soon after we were married. But why should that come as a surprise? Shouldn't we marry someone we have normally and naturally befriended, and not make an artificial separation between a companionship and a romance?

Yet Melanie's reflexive response is exactly the way we often think. Love and romance can be complicated; there are appearances to maintain, secrets to hold and withhold, a public image to consider. Friendship isn't that way; it's comfortable and fun, we think. And long term friendships involve not only trust and dependability, but a measure of realism about one another.

When Hal was a teenager, he and his father looked into a customizing kit which would transform their ancient Volkswagen Beetle with a classic, MG-style sports car body—clamshell fenders, big headlights and all. It was exciting to picture. The red "MG" promised a certain dash and style, highly desirable to a young man (of any age) and pleasant to dream over. That is, until Hal remembered that underneath the chrome and fiberglass, there would always be that humble little VW engine, obediently powering his usual errands to pick up his little sister at school or a bag of groceries on the way home from band practice. The shell was romantic, but it wasn't real.

And that is part of the problem in our relationships. A purely romantic relationship may be all external, depending on a succession of special occasions, best dress, and emotional highs that are full while they last, but aren't sustainable.

Hal's little 1960 VW would never become anything more than that, and it certainly never rose to anything approaching excitement.[1] On the other hand, marriage *can* be both. There is potential for excitement and romance, *and* there can *and should* be a broad foundation of friendship underneath. Someone said we will tolerate things in a friend which we would never allow in a lover. That's backwards; it's an example of the artificial distinction again. It certainly doesn't match the bride's words in the Song. Love is the more comprehensive relationship; it should cover a multitude of sins, as Solomon wrote in the Proverbs and Peter quoted a millennium later.[2] Shouldn't lovers enjoy the same tolerance, grace, forgiveness and trust, as the world expects friends to show?

As we've grown through our first quarter century of matrimony, we've realized that many people struggle with their marriage precisely because of that separation—they have friendships, and they have their spouse, and the two classifications don't match up very well. They don't approach their closest legal and moral relationship, to their husband or wife, with the same interest, enthusiasm, and intentionality that they do for their BFFs and college buddies and co-working relationships.

We'd like to recommend a change to that.

---

1 Not even the *Fahrvergnügen* (Joy of Driving) in 1990 VW ads.
2 Proverbs 10:12, 1 Peter 4:8

## Why We Wrote This

A few years ago, Hal was diagnosed with stage IV cancer. The tumor started in an empty space behind his breastbone, causing few outward symptoms and no sensation or swelling. When a bout of pneumonia led to a chest x-ray and the tumor's discovery, the cancer had already spread to multiple organs and locations. The doctors gave him a little better than a 50-50 chance of survival.

That sort of prognosis makes you sit back and take stock—what sort of legacy will you leave, if you find yourself leaving sooner than you planned? Earlier that year, we had written out our basic view of childrearing and parenting, as detailed as we could make it, and prepared it for publication in book form.[3] We were thankful for that. Whatever happened with this cancer, we knew that our eight children would have an understanding of what we were trying to accomplish in their raising, and why.

But in writing about childrearing, we had stopped at the point of sending our young men off to college or careers. We really hadn't written much about their search for a mate, or how to lay a foundation for a successful marriage, or how to start resolving things if the relationship wandered off course or went sour, somehow.

And while we were speaking in more and more places about the challenges and opportunities of raising boys—after all, folks noticed we had six of them, and they were curious—we were getting questions about broader issues. People were asking for advice about their children's courtships and relationships, or seeking counseling for their own marriage,

---

3 *Raising Real Men: Surviving, Teaching and Appreciating Boys* (Smithfield, N.C: Great Waters Press, 2010)

or wondering how to fix other relationships that weren't working as they should.

We thank God and the staff He placed at Duke University Medical Center that Hal is cancer free now. And this book is our attempt to share with our children, our friends, and anyone else who has an interest, what we've seen and learned and practiced in a friendship of thirty years—and in a marriage for the last twenty-six of them.

## How This Book Is Organized

Each season, Coach Vince Lombardi would open practice with a speech.

"Gentlemen," he would say, holding up the pigskin, "this is a football."

His point, of course, was that success in the game requires a thorough understanding of the fundamentals. Several of our sons have played football, and being linemen, they will all tell you that big plays might score the winning touchdowns, but the big breakthrough plays don't happen if the team doesn't do well with blocking, tackling, and keeping a grip on the ball, play after play after play.

Basic understanding matters. Commitment to fundamental truth, in spite of constant small temptations and distractions, matters. Skill can be learned, and it takes practice. It's true of football, true of life in general, and true of marriage in particular.

When we set out to organize this book, we found the topics didn't follow a neat engineer-pleasing flow diagram, proceeding from point to logical point with occasional branches and junctions. Instead, one topic connects with a dozen others. The naturalist John Muir said, "When one tugs at a single thing in nature, he finds it attached to the rest of the world." Marriage is like that, too, so we looked for a pattern to follow.

The most fundamental truths about marriage are the ones announced when marriage was created:

> ...the LORD God said, "It is *not good that man should be alone; I will make him a helper comparable to him."* 4

> *So God created man in His own image; in the image of God He created him; male and female He created them. Then God blessed them, and God said to them, "Be fruitful and multiply; fill the earth and subdue it; have dominion over the fish of the sea, over the birds of the air, and over every living thing that moves on the earth."*[5]

> *Then God saw everything that He had made, and indeed* it was *very good.*[6]

When God created mankind, as male and female, He had several things in mind—providing companionship for one another, raising up a family, undertaking a mission to cultivate and govern the created world around them, and providing mutual help and support in all the work He had given them to do. He created man, male and female, to represent Him on earth—to be like Him, to carry His image, to reflect His character in some way. And when it was all put together, *behold, it was very good.*

---

4  Genesis 2:18
5  Genesis 1:27-28
6  Genesis 1:31

So we've arranged this book under those headings. You might go directly to the chapter which addresses the need you feel. You might turn the page and go through in order. However you read it, in the end, we hope you will be able to say it's helped you draw your marriage a little closer to that ideal. We hope your marriage is not just good, but *very good*.

*And the LORD God said,*
**"It is not good that the man should be alone..."**

— Genesis 2:18a

# ~ 1 ~

# Leaving and Cleaving

*Therefore shall a man leave his father and his mother, and shall cleave unto his wife: and they shall be one flesh.*

— Genesis 2:24 (KJV)

We were both Christians when we got married, and so were most of our college friends—i.e., the ones in charge of pranks at the reception. Oh, we had the usual good-natured sabotage like the dead chicken on the hood of the car and the Oreo cookies under the windshield wipers when we tried to clear the shaving cream off the glass. We never got every grain of birdseed out of that car). But the graffiti left by high-spirited collegians with a Biblical bent kind of stands out. Cryptic messages like *"1 Cor 7:1!"* (*"It is better to marry than to burn"*) aren't the kind of things your fraternity brothers think up. Neither was the motto, *"Leaving and Cleaving!"* in the back window.

The verse about finally finding a home for all that repressed desire is the easy part. Who knew that the other verse was much harder to implement.

## What The Bible Says

When God created marriage, in its original sinless perfection, He described a tremendous change in relationships. A man would leave his parents and "*cleave*" to his wife, as the old translations say; the modern renderings say "*be joined*" (NKJV, NASB), "*hold fast*" (ESV), or "*be united*" (NIV) to his wife.

Since the passage goes on to address the "one flesh" relationship, it's natural to associate this verse with the mystery of sexual union. That's appropriate as far as it goes, but it's also true this verse addresses the social relationships. When you get married, you transfer your attention and loyalty from your birth family to the new family, specifically your mate.

The word in the Old Testament Hebrew was often used to describe the Israelites' relationship with God, especially in passages which called them to turn their loyalty to Him in active, conscious commitment. There's an element of volition, of will:

> Ye shall walk after the LORD your God, and fear
> Him, and keep His commandments, and obey His
> voice, and ye shall serve Him, and cleave unto Him.[1]

But there is a note of a deep, overwhelming, transforming connection. The term is used to describe pursuit, overtaking, and engagement in battle.[2] It describes the way a disease infiltrates and overpowers the body.[3] It even speaks to the way the dirt clods cling together in the burning sun of drought.[4]

---

[1] Deuteronomy 13:4 (KJV)
[2] Genesis 31:23; Judges 20:42, 45
[3] Deuteronomy 28:21, 60
[4] Job 38:38

So when a man and woman marry, the Bible describes a willful, conscious, determined adherence to one another. They embrace and infiltrate one another so that they can't really be separated. The Bible says the two of them become one flesh, like a single organism which once was two. It's like two handfuls of clay kneaded together by a potter to fashion a single object.

It seems that the peace and harmony we experience with each other in marriage is largely a reflection of how far we've come in merging ourselves together. The friction and division we experience points out the places where we've maintained a separate sense of identity and entitlement.

Now it's true that even when we are deeply united with each other, there is still individuality present. Even if we're one in spirit, there will always be differences of temperament, intellect, and personality. One spouse can grow sick and even die, and the other go on living, without interrupting the love and adherence they felt toward one another. We are created male and female to complement and complete one another, not to transfer parts of our personhood back and forth like strands of DNA until the result is a pair of almost-clones, one with long hair, one with a deep voice.

But in those parts which involve our self-will, self-determination, and self-seeking, God intends for us to grow more focused on our spouse and less on our self.

## There's Theory, and There's Application

Back during the Cold War, there was a story about a political commissar visiting a peasant in a Russian village.

"If you had two houses, Comrade, would you not gladly share the second with your poor neighbor for the glory of your Motherland?" the commissar asked.

"But certainly, Comrade," replied the peasant.

"And if you had two barns?"

"Of course."

"And would you not give your second plough-horse for the service of your impoverished neighbor?"

"Yes, definitely."

"And your second pig?" the commissar asked.

"No, not the pig," replied the peasant.

"No? Why ever not?" asked the puzzled official.

"Well, I actually *have* two pigs," explained the peasant.

It's easy to assent to a principle when the application is just a theory. When it becomes reality, though, the difficulty suddenly arises.

Hal has an easy-going personality and is generally content to give way to Melanie's preferences and wishes in many areas. When we were courting or newlyweds, it seemed only right and gentlemanly to give her the choice of restaurants for an evening out, or let her pick the movie, or follow her tastes in decorating.

One day she was playing the commissar in the story, though, and mentioned Hal's camera.

Suddenly, he felt himself balk. That was *his* camera—something he'd saved for, treasured, carried throughout high school and college and two trips to Europe. Photography was one of his hobbies and he was proud of that camera. He didn't feel ready to sign a joint ownership agreement on *that*.

And so that was precisely where it needed to happen. Realizing the fact only made it more unsettling. Was the camera the second pig in the story? Absolutely. Suddenly, he grasped that it was easy to let the fiancée choose dinner because he didn't really have an opinion either way. That didn't involve any self-sacrifice at all. It was love, but it was cheap. Giving up, even just sharing, the camera was hard.

But that's where we have to consider the principle in real application. Do we really mean it when we speak of being one, or do we block off areas and things and people which we consider our own sacred hunting grounds, and only open them to our beloved for occasional escorted tours? Where are we hiding the second pig?

## Leaving Is Harder

Growing into a true union as husband and wife will take commitment, selflessness, and time, and that's expected. The command to leave father and mother will press hard, right from the start. It doesn't wait. And it's not easy.

Our culture is not making the transition any smoother. One problem is young adults' hesitation to step out of the comfortable, more-or-less undemanding place as their parents' dependents.

According to sociologists, there are five gateways which signify full adult independence: completing your education, moving out of your parents' home, finding a job, finding a mate, and starting a family. In the span of a generation, though, we've seen a significant rise in the time before we leave home, and a sharp trend toward delayed marriage. For example, one out of five American men in their late twenties is still living with his parents today.[5] In Canada, the number of young adults in their twenties still living with their parents went from 27% in 1981 to over 40% in 2011, including more than 60% of men ages 20-24.[6] And since 1970, the median age of first marriage for men has gone from 24 to 28.5 years old, and from 22 to nearly 27 for women—a huge demographic shift.[7]

Certainly in unstable economic times there are situations where young married couples, or even older ones, might share their parents' home for a short time of transition. That may be a plan for bridging across hard circumstances, and not an indefinite arrangement to sponge off Mom and Dad as long as possible. If it's not temporary, though, whether by design or by circumstances, it will make for a difficult balancing act as two generations seek to live together in harmony as adults.

The change in maturation may be because cultural values have shifted and removed much of the stigma from "living in sin." As society has relaxed its approbation against premarital

---

[5] Zhenchao Qian, 2012. "During The Great Recession, More Young Adults Lived with Parents." Census Brief prepared for Project US2010. ‹http://www.s4.brown.edu/us2010›, accessed 5/12/13.

[6] Statistics Canada, 2011 Census.*Living arrangements of young adults aged 20 to 29.* 2011 Census in Brief. Ottawa: Statistics Canada, 2012 (Cat. No. 98-312-X2011003). ‹http://www4.hrsdc.gc.ca/.3ndic.1t.4r@-eng.jsp?i-id=77›, accessed 5/11/13.

[7] U.S. Decennial Census (1890-2000); American Community Survey (2010). See ‹http://www.census.gov/acs›. ‹http://www.census.gov/hhes/socdemo/marriage/data/acs/ElliottetalPAA2012figs.pdf›

sexuality, the age of first marriage has increased five and six years for men and women respectively, and three out of five people have lived with a boyfriend or girlfriend prior to marriage.[8] And if social reaction is your guide and standard, then indeed, why risk a lifelong commitment when a disposable relationship can provide many of the same perks?

There is also a definite slump in the ambition and vision of young people—especially young men—which has led researchers to extend their definition of adolescence into the mid-thirties. Clinical psychologists Joseph and Claudia Allen of the University of Virginia have observed that "twenty-five is the new fifteen," and levels of maturity and adult behavior we once expected of teenagers are becoming rare in people still in their twenties.[9]

Unfortunately, these unbiblical attitudes are permeating even the church.

We recently posted a link on our Facebook page to a news report stating that the majority of children born to women under 30 were now born out of wedlock.[10] We commented how sad this was and we were shocked when people identifying themselves as Christians defended their decisions to have children outside marriage and to delay marriage even

---

[8] Kennedy, Sheela, and Larry Bumpass. "Cohabitation and children's living arrangements: New estimates from the United States." *Demographic Research*. 19. (2008): 1663-1692. Web. 29 Aug. 2012. ‹http://www.demographic-research.org/volumes/vol19/47/19-47.pdf›.

[9] Allen, J., and C.W. Allen. *Escaping the endless adolescence, how we can help our teenagers grow up before they grow old*. First. New York, NY: Ballantine Books, 2010. Print.

[10] Jason DeParle and Sabrina Tavernise, "for Women Under 30, Most Births Occur Outside of Marriage." New York: New York Times, 2/17/12. ‹http://www.nytimes.com/2012/02/18/us/for-women-under-30-most-births-occur-outside-marriage.html?pagewanted=all&_r=0›

after those children were born. This is just wrong, it's the sin of fornication and sadly, it's the children who will pay the price in lack of security.

And where does that leave us with the marriages which *do* occur?

Frankly, it means that those who *are* traditional and moral enough to pursue marriage rather than a "friend with benefits," are approaching the union with less maturity than their age might suggest. And that can bring two complications into the relationship—young spouses who haven't stepped out of their role as children in their parents' homes, and parents who recognize their child's shortcomings and find it difficult to release him or her from parental direction.

The relationship between parent and child is supposed to change as the child reaches adulthood. The Fifth Commandment, which applies to people of all ages, says to *Honor your father and mother*,[11] while the apostle's admonition to *obey your parents in the Lord* is directed specifically to children.[12] We read that as two levels of relationship. While our children are growing up at home, they are commanded to obey—in fact, that is their primary commandment from God, that they learn obedience within their family relationship. As they reach maturity, though, we parents need to shift from a role of direction—do this, don't do that—to one of counseling—have you considered this or that aspect of the decision you face? Hopefully, as we make the transition in our parenting style, our sons and daughters will step out into adult life looking back for advice, rather than straining away to gain their independence.

---

[11] Exodus 20:12

[12] Ephesians 6:1

That independence is necessary, as the husband and wife turn their human loyalty and attention toward one another. You leave your father and mother and cleave, hold fast to, and be joined and united to your spouse.

## How do you achieve this?

Maybe the largest thing is to make a conscious habit of thinking in terms of "we", "us", and "our", rather than "me" and "mine." Listen to yourself when you talk with friends or family. What pronouns do you use the most?

Suddenly, you realize that all of your decisions and desires affect someone else, someone you love more than yourself. This is a great opportunity for growth in maturity as you learn to truly regard someone more highly than yourself.

It's time to define what "we" want to do, what "we" want to be—to formulate a set of real family values and goals; to define what our family will be like. The time before you have children is a great opportunity to talk all this through. The time will be well spent when challenges come. If you've already thought out your principles, then you can weather things more easily because the decisions have been made before the pressure is on.

Perhaps the most challenging part of this, though, is establishing that unity within your new, married family, when your birth family is pulling the other way.

## A New Family

It's strange being on the other side of this. We now have children of marriageable age and we've been thinking through the opinions we formed on this subject when we were the newlyweds.

We decided then that we wanted to form our own family traditions. We wanted to take the best of both our families, and do things our own unique way. Just a few months after we were married, Hal was sent to a duty station over a thousand miles away from our families. That first Christmas felt very lonely when we first contemplated it.

We'll never forget the joy when we received a package from Hal's grandmother containing handmade Christmas ornaments and tree skirt, lights and a "First Christmas" ornament. She's long been in heaven, but her kindness in making our first tree homelike will always be special to us. Then the package from Hal's mother came—a box of ornaments from Hal's childhood! What a gift! We decided then and there we were going to have a great Christmas wherever we were—and we were going to give the same gift of love and independence to our children. In fact, it's been our tradition ever since to choose an "ornament of the year" each Christmas and give one to each of our children, expecting that one day they will take them into their own marriage.

Since we moved back to the Carolinas, within an afternoon's drive of both families, we try to share the holidays with them. It may be a day or two before or after the date, or we may invite family to come celebrate at our home, or we may divide the day between our own family's traditions and dinner with grandmother. But we have established our own traditions that identify the holiday for our children and each other wherever we find ourselves. It's one definite way we define our marriage and our family's unique identity.

## But what happens when the parents don't let go?

It's right and good for the newlyweds to set out on their independent pathway, but what about families which bar the door?

We have heard of parents that actually invited their son over for dinner every night, but not his bride! Others may be less outrageous, but never seem to accept their child's choice of a mate, and instead undermine and criticize at every opportunity.

It's difficult for us to understand those destructive behaviors that seem more determined to break a marriage than to accomplish anything real, but we can see lots of times when even good, well-meaning parents might step into a minefield or cause dissention. It's hard when you miss your children—we've felt it ourselves. One year our oldest was a student in England, and when he was home for the holidays, it was hard not to monopolize his time. Often parental demands are just that—a way of expressing, "I miss you and your part in our family, and I don't want things to change." And a lot of parental meddling is probably loving parents who hate to see their grown children making what they believe to be mistakes. Obviously that's different from purely malicious behavior, and it needs to be addressed differently too.

We've recommended this response for years, "Thanks, Mom (or Dad or Grandma), we'll consider that," repeated as often as necessary. That tells them that you've heard them, you will take their concerns into consideration, and it's your decision. That wonderful phrase works in most family arguments. It's especially effective because often defending your decisions is perceived by family as meaning it's up for discussion and your mind can be changed. If you've made a firm decision, just respond with "Thank you, we'll consider that," and wait until they have genuine questions to help them understand.

The most important thing is to respond with a united front. No matter whose idea it was, once both of you have heard it, unless the husband stops it (remember in the Old Testament a husband could annul a wife's commitment if he did so the first time he heard of it), it is now "our" decision. A whole lot of family conflict will be avoided if you start all announcements with "We've decided..."

This is a real opportunity for a husband to show his protection of his wife. It's not unusual for family members to gang up on a wife and challenge her about something the couple is doing, whether it's having another child, extended breastfeeding, or homeschooling. It's true even if they're upset about something the husband is doing! She needs to be able to say, "If you're that concerned, please bring it up with [husband], it's his final decision." Her husband should back her up in this, and openly say, "Yes, we've decided to..." especially if it's *his* birth family involved.

Although all the comic strips and situation comedies laugh about the wife's mother as the awful mother-in-law, we've found in talking to couples over the years that it is much more often the husband's parents that a couple has conflict with. This is probably because you raise a daughter knowing that one day she'll marry and she'll answer to her husband then. On the other hand, the thought is not as ingrained with a son—yes, he's married, but he has no new authority figure—or so it seems. His new authority is the Lord Himself, as the son becomes the head of his own household. That may be a little harder for parents to grasp. And truly, it's partly due to the very serious problem of men being unprepared for independence at all. If your son goes from basement-dwelling gamer to husband, it's hard to take him seriously.

This makes it very important for the husband to be aware of what's going on and to intervene and take responsibility if his wife is feeling attacked. Often, if the husband will simply step up and say, "This is our decision, let's leave it at that," they will! His wife will never forget it, either!

But what should you do if you've tried polite explanations and you've tried taking responsibility, firmness, and changing the subject and still nothing is working? The best option at that point may be to get out of the situation and let everyone cool down a bit. That could be anything from "Let's take a walk, Honey, I need to work off some of Mom's great food," to "I'm sorry, Dad, but something's come up and we're going to have to head home a couple of days early" (that "something" may have been somebody's temper). When the whole family gathers again, whether it's a half hour or half a year later, it may be easy to redirect the conversation to areas of agreement and appreciation.

In the ultimate extreme, when you just can't find a way of life that allows for peace with the relations and a safe bond with your mate, it may be you need to move away for a time. We have terrific families who've been a great blessing to us, but it was probably a good thing that military duty took us far away for our first few years of marriage. It forced us to develop our own family traditions and ways of doing things, and to focus on building our new family. When we were finally able to move back to the Carolinas many years later, we were more secure, lots more mature, and able to build a healthy relationship with our families. For a family caught in a toxic situation, a move like that may be more than just helpful—it may be a marriage-saver.

When all is said and done, leaving your family doesn't mean physical distance, it means rather changing the focus of your primary attention and loyalty to your wife and children. It doesn't mean ceasing to honor your parents, but it does mean that you no longer obey them. That leaves you free to do what you believe is right for your family, but to do it in love. We should always show respect to our parents, listening carefully (and patiently, if necessary) to their advice, instructing our children to do the same, and disagreeing, if we must, in a respectful way. When we are tempted to be short with our own parents, we try to think about how we want our children to treat us in front of our grandchildren and act accordingly.

Similarly, cleaving to your mate means a lot more than the physical union. It means clinging to them so closely that there is more *us* than *me* or *you* in the equation. That takes a conscious decision to choose unity over winning, selflessness over selfishness, and love over self-indulgence. It's also a big blessing to have someone else caring for us, watching out for our needs, trying to please us. It's a lot better than looking out for yourself.

# ~ 2 ~

# How To Be Married To Your Best Friend

*Do not forsake your friend and your father's friend ...*
— Proverbs 27:10 (ESV)

*His mouth is most sweet, Yes, he is alto-*
*gether lovely.* **This is my beloved, And this**
*is* **my friend**, *O daughters of Jerusalem!*
— Song of Solomon 5:16

Shortly before we were married, a friend gave us a cross-stitch motto, "Marriage means never saying goodbye to your best friend."

That's the ideal, isn't it? That your mate would be your very best friend. That's the way we felt about each other then and that's the way we feel today. What's more, this is something you can decide to do. It's something you *ought* to do.

Sometimes people invest more care and intention into their friendships than they do their love affairs. They stick by a friend in spite of his shortcomings, they exercise more toleration and forgiveness of their friend than their lover, they share confidences with their friend but carefully shield them from their romantic interest. But can this be right? When the husband and wife are said to be "one flesh," how can they hold closer relationships outside their marriage?

What if you weren't friends when you married or don't feel that way now? It's easy to talk about friendship and marriage when you feel the way we do, that we truly *did* join hands with our best friend at our wedding. But what if you feel differently about your own spouse—either your first love cooled, or your relationship was something different than "friendship" at the outset? Where do you go from there?

Simple: You decide to befriend your spouse.

## Why the dichotomy (lover vs. friend)?

If the ideal relationship is both friend and lover, why would we ever choose differently? Or if we didn't make a deliberate choice, why would we allow any other form of relationship to rise up between us and our mates? Why does friendship "have to be" something different than romance?

Part of it may be the world's tendency to try and disconnect the things which God designed to go together. When the Pharisees tried to trap Jesus in a controversy over divorce, He pointed them to the account of Creation, saying that husband and wife *"are no longer two but one flesh. Therefore what God has joined together, let not man separate."*[1]

We can look around our neighborhood, even within our churches, and find that divisive mentality infects much more than the issue of divorce. The Sexual Revolution of the sixties promoted the separation of sexual expression from the safe harbor of marriage. Since the 1930's, the Protestant churches have allowed or even promoted the separation of sexual fulfillment and childbearing, as things which are tangentially connected only.

---

[1] Matthew 19:6

And culturally speaking, somehow we seem to put friendship and romance in separate compartments—with marriage in yet another.

## Compartmentalized

The world views three separate compartments of our relationship lives:

| Friendship | Romance | Marriage |
|---|---|---|
| Talk | Love and Sex | Kids and Housework |
| Fun | Excitement | Routine |
| Leisure | Special Events | Work |
| Shared Interests | Shared Fantasies | Shared Duties |
| Wants | Desires | Needs |
| Privacy | Discovery | Knowledge |
| Individuality | Jealousy | Complacency |
| Appreciation | Pursuit | Possession |
| Casual Clothes | Formal Clothes | Comfortable Clothes |

The world's friendship is centered on leisure time spent with people who share our interests. It involves casual clothes and casual conversation, and individuality is respected and desired. There is some privacy, and our friends know only what we choose to reveal to them. We appreciate our friends; by and large the relationship is fun and relaxed.

Romance is something different, though. Instead of mere appreciation, romance involves pursuit. Instead of just shared fun, there is excitement, and why not? Romance is about love (however defined—and usually there's sex in the equation, or the anticipation of it). Shared interests give place to shared fantasies; the casual clothes are replaced by more formal attire, as leisure time is invested in special events. The simple wants of friendship become desires; the admiration of individuality quickens to a quest for discovery of one another, and jealousy too.

Ah, then, *marriage*. Marriage gets short shrift—even while our culture is still structured around the marriage tradition, the institution is seen as something of a buzzkill, a rich mine for night club comedians. Marriage is about stability, routine, and work. It's about shared responsibilities, like caring for children, and it focuses on prosaic needs more than shared passion and the thrill of exploration. Discovery is over and a comfortable, complacent knowledge—even predictability—is the expectation. Now that we possess one another, the coat and tie and formal gown are put away for the slouchy comfort of old shoes and worn out sweats.

Or so the world would say. How many magazines aimed at men or at women headline every cover with tips for spicing up the dreary routines of stolid, long-term relationships? How many books and movies are produced each year with the baseline premise, "If only I wasn't trapped in harness with him or her..." How many young couples are counseled by friends and family to have their fun before they settle down because *you know how it will be, when you're old married folks.*

## We don't accept that...

God created us as eternal souls, personalities which go on forever. In the early days of the world, a couple might live together as husband and wife for centuries. *They* didn't die of boredom.

So why shouldn't you find your mate your best friend? Why can't your old, comfortable, married self be delighted at the thought of spending time with your spouse? Why shouldn't there be shared interest as well as shared fantasies and responsibilities?

It seems to us that you can have it all. You can become best friends with your mate. You can have what we call "The Romantic Friendship of Marriage."

---

**The Romantic Friendship of Marriage**

*Love and sex, communication,*
  *children, and work fill our days.*

*We have fun, excitement, and routine,*
  *depending on the day and time.*

*We are companions in our leisure time,*
  *work, and at special events.*

*We have shared interests, shared dreams,*
  *and shared responsibilities.*

*Our wants, desires, and needs are met together.*

*We have privacy from the world, secret knowl-*
  *edge of each other, and continued discovery.*

*Our individuality is celebrated, We jealously guard*
  *our marriage, and we rest in security.*

*We enjoy appreciating, pursuing,*
  *and possessing one another.*

*We are happy together in comfortable clothes,*
  *work clothes, and all dressed up.*

---

## Moral hazard

Part of the problem may be the concept economists call "moral hazard." The basic principle is that if I believe someone is committed to a relationship, I can take a risk that there will be no consequence if I indulge myself in a bit of misbehavior at their expense. A businessman who bought the damage waiver when he picked up his rental car at the airport might be less cautious about where he parks. A family which has met its insurance deductible for the year might choose to request elective surgery rather than just live with an irritating but non-threatening condition.

It happens in our relationships, too. A wife in a stable marriage might bank on her husband's commitment and continue with a habit she knows annoys him. A husband with a stressful job might let his frustrations out on his family because he's confident they love him enough to put up with his irritability. It's tempting to cut corners.

In most cases, we probably escape serious consequences, just as the carefree rental car driver usually does—but at the hidden cost of weakening the relationship. That's why we might think a bit wistfully of our dating or courtship days, comparing them unfavorably to the present. Now that the marriage is safe and secure, comfortable and mundane, we get lazy or might even be indulging a little moral hazard.

Why was courtship different than marriage? When we were romancing each other, we were on our best behavior. We took care to dress extra nicely, watch our tongues, and show appreciation and care for the other person. *Then*, the hunt was on, and whether you felt like the pursuer or the prize, you both were on your toes. It was the time for courtesy, forethought, even gallantry, as we sought to win each other's hearts.

Is that right, though? We're not talking primarily about the things that make us say, "My, he's let himself go to seed," but the deeper character issues. Where is the consideration? What about the self-sacrifice, patience, and occasional indulgences you once knew from the other? Maybe we married folks are taking too much for granted.

That's why we might be treating our spouse differently today than when we were fiancés. But why do we treat our mates differently than our friends? Probably because we let ourselves. Either we never took the time to develop a friendship with the one we would marry, or we just let ourselves drift apart. We let ourselves become emotionally distant while geographically close, like co-workers or roommates. We work together or live together, but really have nothing in common.

Regardless of the reason, there's no time like the present to start making your mate your best friend.

## What makes a good friendship?

What makes a great friendship? Shared interests? Liking the same things? Listening to one another? Being there through thick and thin? Loyalty? Dependability? Consideration? Really, all of those things.

The Word says to have a friend, you must show yourself friendly.[2] This is true in marriage, as well. If you want to be married to your best friend, then you have to be friends with the one you wed. And to make friends anew, you need to think and act like friends would.

### Common interests

One of the first things which draws us to our friends is a shared interest. Cultivating these attractions is a powerful way to build our relationship.

---

2 Proverbs 18:24

Naturally, we had some shared interests which brought us together as friends long before we were romantically attracted, but as we were courting and after we were married, we did some of this "mutual-interest development," too.

For example, many boys have an electric train at some point in their childhood, but Hal grew into a real railroad buff—not only building models of trains, structures, and interesting scenery, but researching long-dead railroad lines, staking out trackside photo shoots when steam engines came through town, breathing the smell of coal smoke and creosote like it was fine perfume. It was a passion that Melanie didn't bring into the relationship. She really wasn't interested at all.

On the other hand, Melanie brought wildflowers—and not just a woman's interest in beautiful blossoms, but a biologist's appreciation for genus and species and habitat an d taxonomy. Her college studies took her into the field to collect samples in the wild, and she grew to love the tiny hidden things in the roadsides and ditches. Early in our relationship, while we were both in college, she would roam the mountains with her plant press in the car, looking for examples of Appalachian flora to complete her course requirements.

We wanted to spend time with each other, so we indulged each other's interests. Hal went on plant collecting expeditions with Melanie, and she listened to his discourses on transportation history and civil engineering as they rode through the hills.

Surprisingly, we found a growing appreciation for subjects we'd never considered. We discovered wildflowers grew profusely along railroad embankments. Melanie began to see geography and history in the names on the sides of passing boxcars at grade crossings. Hal began to stop alongside the road to harvest prairie coneflowers and spiderwort to transplant into our yards.

We built a model railroad together and camped out at the Wildflower Pilgrimage in the Tennessee mountains.

In the beginning, neither of us had much interest in the other subject. But because Hal loved trains, Melanie began to love them, too. Because Melanie loved flowers, Hal grew to appreciate them as well. As our knowledge grew, we began to love them for themselves, and for the value our mate attached to them. Each hobby became our own.

## Discover new things together

You can also discover totally new things together. Both of us are avid readers, and we've always shared favorite books (some we adopt as our own, some we don't). Occasionally though we'd find an author who was new to both of us, and when we'd both read the book, we'd discuss it. That's how we found some of our shared favorites that we eagerly collect today. We've done the same with quirky restaurants, new cuisines, and old movies.

We've adopted each others' ancestors, in a sense. When one of our sons visited the ancient castle of Hal's forefathers in Scotland, Melanie was as pleased as Hal was. When Hal spent a business trip weekend in a state archive and located the grave of Melanie's multiple-great grandfather, he was delighted to discover his wife's colorful Civil War ancestor. We are like the character in *The Pirates of Penzance* who bought an estate with an occupied crypt, saying, "I don't know whose ancestors they *were*, but I know whose ancestors they *are*."[3]

[3] Sullivan, Arthur, and W. S. Gilbert. "Act II, Scene 1." *The Pirates of Penzance, Or, The Slave of Duty an Entirely Original Comic Opera in Two*

You can choose to involve yourself in whatever your mate likes to do, even if it offers no attraction to you but your mate's interest. You may be surprised to find after a while that it becomes one of *your* favorite things, but regardless, you will have knit one more bond between you.

You can also build shared interests by doing projects together. Hal's parents refinished antique furniture as a hobby, and when we were married, Hal's mom gave us a few pieces in pretty serious need of attention. One piece was a low pine dresser that we wanted to use as a changing table. As we worked together stripping the paint and selecting the new finish, we had the enjoyment of a useful project, gained more ideas and experiences to talk about, and had a tangible expression of our work together when we were done. We still use that pine dresser for other purposes now, and we feel happy whenever we see it.

## Separate Interests?

Do we still have our own interests? Yes, because we're still individuals. Hal still reads more straight history and biography than Melanie; she reads more fiction and classics than he does. Melanie experiments in the kitchen more, while Hal is satisfied knowing how to cook five or six set meals and make sandwiches the rest of the time. The crucial thing is that we do share one another's interests in many areas, and that strengthens our friendship as we enjoy them together.

There is a cautionary aspect to consider, though. The time you invest pursuing a separate interest may be attention you take away from your family. There are widows to blogging and videogames just as surely as there are football widows and wives abandoned for the corporate ladder. There are

Acts. London: Chappell, 1879.

husbands feeling lonely and neglected for the sake of social media, scrapbooking, or volunteer work. You simply have to be aware of the balance of time spent apart from each other and the time which you share.

We found a middle route one time. We are both regular bookworms, but in the early days of marriage we hated to turn away from this delightful new living arrangement to bury ourselves in silent reading. Instead, we started reading to one another while we worked or drove. This became a new hobby of ours, and a few years later we discovered audiobooks, allowing us to share the story when it was too dark or the passenger was too tired to read. To this day, we are prone to sharing a book, keeping two markers inside as we individually read the same volume a day or two apart. We've even found duplicate copies of the same title in used bookstores and read the book simultaneously.

We have purposed to *be* friends. We take the time to talk, to visit, to share projects, and to do things we enjoy together. When you make your mate your best friend, you always have a friend along!

## Maybe you let some things go

There are times when the cause of building the relationship may suggest lettings some things go. This isn't the kind of conscientious reform like the parent who gives up smoking when his first child is born, where the relationship drives you to quit a habit which should have been abandoned already. Sometimes you will find it expedient to release a perfectly inoffensive part of your life for the greater good of the relationship.

When we were in college, Hal was gradually building up a stereo sound system. In the days before downloadable mp3 files, this meant selecting and purchasing a quality turntable for the vinyl albums which were the foundation of a music system.[4] A good cassette deck was needed to make the copies used for day-to-day playback (and also to enjoy in the car). An AM/FM radio tuner served as the system's amplifier and mixer, and after three upgrades, a pair of massive floor speakers served as end tables beside the dorm-room sofa. Though it was far from being the most elaborate, powerful, or expensive sound system in the neighborhood, but it was an integral part of daily life in the student world. Hal and his roommate used to joke about "the life support system," since the stereo components would often be connected before the furniture and books were unloaded. If someone was in the room and awake, the music was on—period.

Melanie's world was starkly different. Easily distracted by noise and afflicted by roommates whose musical tastes were, well, very different than her own, Melanie preferred to save radio and tapes for the car.

How could these be reconciled? Hal could have inflicted his musical habits on Melanie and trusted that she loved him enough to put up with them. He could have retreated into a world of headphones, which would have preserved Melanie's peaceful surroundings but deprived her of his company and interaction—particularly if he clamped on the headphones as frequently as he was accustomed to hearing his stereo back at college.[5]

---

[4] We *told* you we were dinosaurs.

[5] It was interesting to observe the change in the dormitory environment when our oldest son started college. The relative silence was remarkable, compared to the world of competing stereo systems we remembered from our undergraduate days. The iPod and its earbuds had effectively ended that aural duel—at least during the week, it seemed.

Or he could do what he eventually did—decide the company of his bride was more important, not to mention more interesting, than whatever was on the radio or tape deck. The speakers found a home with Melanie's brother (still in college at the time) and the other components were put in storage.

Interestingly enough, it wasn't the end of music in the house, just a change in the way it was experienced. Some years later as we began homeschooling our oldest child, Melanie discovered a series of recorded biographies of great composers with samples of their music. We began listening to these with our children and not only gained a new enjoyment of classical music, we discovered the work of several unfamiliar composers *together*—one of those shared experiences, again.

## The place of outside friendships

Does marriage affect our relationships with our other friends? You bet. Marriage changes everything, and it can't be denied.

The motto our friend gave us was a little poignant because she had been Melanie's best female friend for many years. They had talked and visited, laughed and cried together, worried out relationships and life in the "college and career" years, and leaned on one another even though hundreds of miles separated them...not a trivial thing in the days before text messaging and email.

When marriage came, though, the relationship had to change a bit. Melanie no longer looked to her old friend as her main counselor and confidante, but confided in her new husband, Hal. Now Melanie was no longer as available to drop everything and talk for hours as she once was. The time that Hal was home from work was precious to her and she didn't want to spend all that on the phone. Her friend is still dear now decades later, but the transition was a hard thing for both to adjust to.

## Marriage has to come first

One of the first principles of friendships is that your marriage has got to come before any outside relationships. That means you no longer do just whatever you feel like doing, but base your decisions on how "we" have decided to spend our time and resources. Your friends may resent that, especially if they are single or not in wholehearted marriages, and they may try to make you feel guilty for putting your relationship with your mate first. Don't fall for it. You are supposed to be cleaving to your mate; it's right to put that friendship ahead of all others.

## The first virtue of the Proverbs 31 woman

Another key to friendship is trust. Can you share your inner concerns and fears, and know they will be held in confidence? Can your friend depend on you to keep a secret as well?

Proverbs 31 describes the virtuous woman (and excellent wife) whose worth is "far above rubies." The very first characteristic is her concern for her husband's affairs:

> *The heart of her husband trusts in her, and he*
> *will have no lack of gain. She does him good,*
> *and not harm, all the days of her life.*[6]

---

[6] Proverbs 31:11-12 (ESV). The KJV rendering is more familiar, starting with verse 10: *Who can find a virtuous woman? for her price is far above rubies. The heart of her husband doth safely trust in her, so that he shall have no need of spoil.*

Early on we made a commitment to trust one another, and we had to live up to the trust our mate was placing in us. Financial trust is one thing, but emotional trust is much deeper. It starts by protecting confidences. We made it a principle to never tell our friends something which would embarrass or hurt our mate if they heard us share it. This takes some discipline if you have a sense of humor and love to make folks laugh; we often have to stop and think, "Wait—this story may be funny, but will it make my mate look foolish? How would they feel if I made them the butt of this joke?"

## Only make fun with permission

Sometimes the humor is okay, if you clear it beforehand. We had a famous camping trip with an unexpected 2 a.m. downpour that had a sleepy Hal checking weather reports on his cell phone, disbelieving the sound of rain pounding on the tent. At dawn our 5-year-old daughter was wailing in terror at the granddaddy-longlegs clinging to the outside of the mosquito netting, while Melanie the biologist tried to comfort her by explaining they were *arachnids* but not really *spiders*. Both of us had a turn looking a bit silly, but we both laugh at it now and we share those moments freely—with each other's permission.

But other times it's become clear that it would hurt our beloved to share a terribly amusing story—even if we didn't mean any harm or disrespect by it. That makes it off limits. By the way, we give our children the same respect—if a story hurts their dignity or feelings, we don't share it...period.[7]

---

[7] This was very important to us when we wrote our first book, *Raising Real Men*. We didn't want the personal stories we shared in the book be a source of embarrassment to any of our children, so we let each of our sons read the manuscript long before it went into print. If they

## Don't use humor to harm one another

Sometimes, to be frank, our humor may not be meant to be funny at all. It is shocking to hear what some people will share about their spouse in the form of a prayer request—whether privately or in a meeting of the church. If you really need prayer support in a matter that reflects poorly on your spouse, you need to err on the side of vagueness and generality rather than violate the trust you have. "Please pray for my husband, he's been so down," is a lot less troubling than, "Would you pray my husband would get off his lazy tush and work? All he does is mope!" Respect and trust is a cornerstone of a real relationship.

## Dangerous Friendships

There is real dynamite, and a book of matches, where independent friendships involve the opposite sex. It may be an old high school friend, a co-worker, a fellow member of the community band or church choir, but legitimate interactions can start to cross boundaries if you're not very, very careful.

In our wide-open society, we will always be walking a fine line when we are dealing with outside acquaintances. Our reputations and our marriage may be staked on that line, and yet it may be impossible to completely avoid. At different times in his career Hal was assigned a college student to train during summer months; even in the male-dominated business of engineering and maintenance, sometimes those students were female. Business protocol dictates that male and female co-workers must be treated the same, and a collegial atmosphere is encouraged. However, when the student was a young woman, Hal had to maintain a careful distance

objected to any of the stories as presented, we either revised the account—dropping the name, for example—or replaced the story altogether.

to prevent a professional relationship from becoming more personal. That meant never thinking of them as anything but "student," limiting conversations to the business at hand, and avoiding casual socializing. Melanie, on the other hand, had many non-romantic friendships with guys growing up; perhaps the Lord was preparing her to be the mother of six boys and spend almost two decades as the only female in a house full of males.

Friends of the opposite sex present real challenges. Whatever the level of friendship, there need to be safeguards in place to prevent temptation. We make it a practice to never be alone with a member of the opposite sex—if we're never alone, there can never be an accusation of a physical impropriety. We need to be *doubly* cautious about confiding in opposite-gender friends. Many people have fallen into the trap of sharing marital problems with a sympathetic ear only to find themselves drawn into an extramarital relationship. If you need marriage counseling, you need to be talking to someone of the same sex, or the two of you find someone to talk to as a couple.

## Feeling alone in the world wide web?

This extends to social media, too. We've been delighted to recover friendships which lay dormant since we left high school or college, or to discover what happened to favorite coworkers or old neighbors. We've also found some relationships which were better *not* to renew. The Web offers a false sense of privacy, and while we might steer clear of pornography and online dating sites, we can still be drawn into indiscretion or worse.

When we were just a few years into our marriage, right as the Internet was beginning to take off, we watched as a

Christian leader we respected fell into an adulterous relationship. There was nothing new about that, except for the first time we saw how it could start with a simple email conversation. It was two or three years before we had our first Internet account, but we decided at the outset to keep one another accountable whenever we did get online. For several years, we shared a single email address, and only divided it when Hal's work with the state homeschool association began to bury our limited personal correspondence with incoming messages. To this day, our policy is to share all our passwords for anything online—from our email provider to Facebook to purchasing accounts at any number of retailers. We keep accountability software on all our computers and Internet-capable phones, so no one has a secret place to cultivate an evil habit or the wrong sort of friendships. And we have taught our sons, as they've reached young adulthood, to embrace the same sort of transparency and accountability in their lives and relationships, too.

## Communication

One of the foundations of friendship, along with shared interests, common experiences, and trust, is communication. Friendship takes investment of your time and your heart. You have to stay in touch. It takes effort, thoughtfulness, and courtesy. Words are unbelievably powerful: the Bible tells us, *There is one whose rash words are like sword thrusts, But the tongue of the wise brings healing.*[8] A sword sounds pretty drastic an analogy, but a few chapters later, it even says, *Death and life are in the power of the tongue.*[9] We need to be aware of how we are communicating with our mates and choose to use words that edify and encourage, while avoiding those that tear down and destroy.

[8] Proverbs 12:18 (ESV)
[9] Proverbs 18:21 (ESV)

This is one of the first places we let our relational guard slip. When we give ourselves permission to let the tongue off its leash, to relax our hold on the reins, our communication rapidly degenerates. We discover some incident of spousal stupidity (we all have our shining moments) and we make accusations, call them unflattering names, and express our judgment: *Wow, that was idiotic.* Instead, we should have chosen to overlook the transgression, forgive them of their failure, and maybe even treat them the way we want to be treated.

Jesus warned us that by our own words we are justified or condemned.[10] I think many of us would not want to hear all the words we've spoken to our spouses as justification or condemnation of ourselves. The book of James, too, is full of warnings about the power of the tongue. We can't just brush off the issue as "just words."

## No Mind Reading Expected

As dangerous as they are, we have to use words. Non-verbal communication only goes so far.

We have to make sure we say things clearly, instead of expecting our mates to read our minds. Years ago, we were deep cleaning an apartment prior to moving, and we stumbled across an all-night marathon of *Dick Van Dyke Show* re-runs on TV. One episode opened with Rob and Laura riding in a car, obviously out of sorts with each other. When Rob asked Laura why she was so upset, she would only respond, "*You know!*" The whole half hour followed Rob's clumsy attempts to deduce what was driving a wedge in their evening, with

---

[10] Matthew 12:37

his wife only dropping occasional clues between the emotional sniffles.[11]

Like much of that series, the episode was funny because the relationship struggle was so recognizable—and while the situation is familiar, it's not funny in real life.

When the prophet Samuel was sent by God to anoint a successor to the faithless King Saul, God warned him not to be distracted by externalities, for *man looks on the outward appearance, but the Lord looks on the heart.*[12] How often to we, like Laura Petri, expect our mates to know what we are thinking, or jump to conclusions by thinking we know what *they* are thinking. Is that confusing enough?

We homeschool our children and operate a business from home, too, so we have plenty of opportunity to work on our communication skills. Occasionally one of our older sons will take offense if we ask, during the usual school hours, "What are you working on?" We have to remind them that from where we parents stand or sit, all we can see is that they are engaged on their laptop. They might be studying a computer-based literature course, writing an essay, or drilling themselves on Chinese vocabulary; on the other hand, they might be shopping for car parts, watching TV re-runs, or playing games on Facebook. Without more information, all we know for certain is the laptop is open.

The same way, if we don't make an effort to reveal our thoughts to one another, there's not much chance we'll really understand what's going on behind our mate's eyes. Certainly there is a time to speak and a time to keep silence, but when

---

[11] "My Husband Is a Check Grabber." *The Dick Van Dyke Show.* Wtr. Carl Reiner. Perf. Dick Van Dyke and Mary Tyler Moore. 1963.
[12] 1 Samuel 16:7 (ESV)

we make a practice of bottling up our inner lives, we could be preventing our mate from fulfilling God's commands.

Really? Yes, really. Paul admonished the believers in Rome to *Rejoice with those who rejoice, and weep with those who weep.* They were to *Be of the same mind toward one another.*[13] How is that even possible unless we share our feelings and draw back the veil from our minds? How can your mate be faithful to the command to *Bear one another's burdens, and so fulfill the law of Christ,*[14] if you consistently refuse to explain what those burdens are?

Although you always retain your own individuality, with different gifts and weaknesses, you need to be thinking about "The Marriage." You need to have your relationship always in mind as important factor in your life. When you have a disagreement, you aim to come to a conclusion that is a win for both of you, as a married couple, the same way you are careful to avoid blurting out things that would wreck a valuable friendship. Instead of competing to win an argument, we should be striving to outdo one another in doing good.

## Invest time in communicating

Take the time to catch up when you've been apart. Talk through your days. Share your opinions. Share your heart and seek out theirs. Be a safe haven where they can talk through their concerns without fear of judgment. Let them know you are on their side—always. That's extremely powerful and your mate will never forget it when you are there for them, a safe harbor, when they feel attacked or let down by the world.

---

13 Romans 12:15-16
14 Galatians 6:2

Profitable communication, though, requires vulnerability. It requires that you let down your guard. It's important to remember that the two of you are not two warring kingdoms, but rather you are the monarchs of the kingdom of your family and disagreements are therefore civil wars. Civil wars are always bloody, heart-breaking affairs, too.

Instead, whether you feel it or not, you should be showing even more love and respect for your mate as you do your other friends. If you express it in whatever way you can, you will begin to feel it more and more until it's no effort at all. We can choose to enjoy one another. Choose to see each other as our best friends. This is really, seriously one of the most satisfying things you will ever do. Make your mate your best friend.

*And the LORD God said,...*
*"I will make him*
**a helper comparable to him."**

— Genesis 2:18b

# ~ 3 ~

## In Sickness and In Health

*"I was sick and you visited Me...assuredly, I say
to you, inasmuch as you did it to one of the
least of these My brethren, you did it to Me."*
— Matthew 25:36, 40

It's funny how things turn out differently than you expect. When we were newly married, Melanie was very conscious that she might have to deal with Hal becoming seriously ill or even dying. Her father had died in a car accident at 38 years old and Hal's father of a heart attack at 44. Melanie used to sleep with her hand on Hal in the hopes that she'd wake if he stopped breathing. She prayed desperately for his safety whenever he left the house. She worried about his weight, fearful he'd have heart trouble. It took a long time to realize that our joyful marriage was not going to be just a brief interlude before grief.

And as it turned out, Hal was the first to be challenged to love in sickness.

At the very start of our first pregnancy, Melanie began bleeding, and our obstetrician put her on bed rest and medication to try and avert a possible miscarriage. After several weeks, that crisis was past, and the days passed normally until her blood pressure began to climb dangerously. Back to bed she was sent for several more weeks. We're thankful we didn't know that was going to be the easiest pregnancy!

The second was much harder; we discovered that Melanie had a condition which would bring about labor very early and quite painlessly, so to head off a premature birth at 20 weeks, Melanie was put on bed rest in the Trendelenburg position, with her feet elevated nearly a foot higher than her head. Tilted upside down in the bed for ten weeks, Melanie couldn't even stand long enough to shower; Hal bathed her in bed, even washing her long hair with a large plastic bucket.

It was a hard time for us all. Melanie, used to being a competent, self-reliant leader, had to learn patience while others waited on her, dependent on the thoughtfulness of others and helpless when she wanted to be busy. A friend moved into our spare bedroom and cared for Melanie during the day, and in the evening, Hal was welcomed home from work to a wild toddler, a tired-out friend, and a cranky, bedridden wife.

Even amid the stress, there were funny scenes. Melanie has never forgotten the angst of noticing a pair of dirty underwear on the floor when church ladies were at the door. What to do? *What to do?* She wasn't supposed to get out of bed at all, but oh, the humiliation! She tried all kinds of things to try to reach them to no avail. Melanie finally jumped out of bed for just a second to grab them, but then felt guilty for days!

As we learned how to manage the situation, subsequent pregnancies became a little less burdensome, but they were all marked by months of medications, partial or full bedrest and anxiety. During every pregnancy, Hal cooked and cleaned and supported the family—at least until the boys got old enough to take over the cooking and cleaning. Melanie says that he never complained, no matter how hard it got.

That example energized her when Hal was diagnosed with advanced cancer in January of 2010. A family-wide bout of flu settled in Hal's lungs and ended up as pneumonia; the diagnostic X-rays disclosed a fist-sized tumor hidden behind his breastbone—Hodgkin's lymphoma, growing with few external symptoms until it had spread to his liver, spleen, and other areas.

"Although I was terrified for my beloved Hal's life," she said later, "I couldn't wait to show him the tender love and care he'd shown me through pregnancy after pregnancy. He was my example!" The course of treatment took him through six months of chemotherapy with its side effects, followed by radiation and months of recovery. Through it all, Melanie carried the emotional burden for herself and all our family and friends, shielding Hal from worries and well-meant but unhelpful advice. She worked harder herself and organized our children to pick up Hal's responsibilities when weakness, nausea, and a depressed immune system prevented him from carrying out his usual duties for the family.

## Love is about doing, not feeling

One of our favorite definitions of love is to put someone else's needs ahead of your own. Paul entreated the church at Philippi to be *like-minded, having the same love,* being *of one accord, of one mind,* and *in lowliness of mind, let each esteem others better than himself.*[1] It's a recurring theme in Paul's letters. In his message to the Romans, *brotherly love* is characterized by *giving preference to one another.*[2] To Ephesus, he wrote to be *longsuffering, bearing with one another in love,* as they were *submitting to one another in the fear of God.*[3] True

---

[1] Philippians 2:2-3
[2] Romans 12:10
[3] Ephesians 4:2, 5:21

love, he wrote elsewhere, is patient, kind, and doesn't demand its own way.[4]

When sickness comes to our marriage, as it eventually will, we get tested in our commitment to that principle. It may not be a disastrous pregnancy or a diagnosis of cancer; it may be as simple as a week of the flu or a nasty stomach bug. It may not be either spouse but a child or an elderly relative. Whether it's life-threatening or just unpleasantly inconvenient, it's an opportunity to demonstrate true love in every dimension. When you find yourself carrying most of the load of a married team, or when you find yourself prevented from fulfilling your normal responsibilities and dreading to become a burden, it helps to remember that the trials you're facing are part of God's school of Christlike love. It's your chance to really prove you really love your mate, hour by hour and day by day.

## Planning for Problems

Often the onset of a time of illness is a surprise. We knew Hal was sick, but pneumonia and a couple of weeks of rest and antibiotics were all we expected. Until our third pregnancy, we had no idea of Melanie's underlying condition, and every difficulty came as a shock. In both cases, though, once the diagnosis was in and the course of treatment laid out, we had some idea of the troubles we would face. If it's something you've seen before—like recurring pregnancy challenges—you can predict what's just over the horizon.

At that point, it really helps to sit down and make plans as soon as you know what you're up against. There will likely be some re-ordering of priorities—hopefully no more than a

---

[4] 1 Corinthians 13:4-5 (ESV)

temporary derangement—and you'll need to figure out what can possibly be set aside. There won't be time to do everything.

One thing which will make an appearance quickly is the financial question. If the illness confronting you is more than a short-term discomfort, you'll need to figure out the impact on your budget. Should you reduce expenses in some areas? Do you need to pull money out of savings or a retirement account?

Or is the situation more dire still?

When our daughter Katie was just two weeks old, her medical bills passed the ten thousand dollar mark in the course of a single afternoon. It was a bolt from the blue.

Katie had a normal birth and appeared to be completely healthy, but several days after we brought her home, Melanie noticed the baby was breathing too fast when she nursed. A respiratory virus had been going around and Melanie was concerned that Katie might have been exposed, so she took her in to our family physician.

When the doctor walked in, he looked over the tiny patient and said, "Oh, I'm sure she's fine; she looks great!" When he placed his stethoscope to her chest, though, his eyebrows shot right up. "It's too fast to count!" he gasped, and shouted for the EKG machine. Katie's heart rate was 276, and within minutes the doctor was on the phone to Life Flight.

Four years later, Katie's doing fine, but that newborn spent weeks in and out of ICU, then had two years of dangerous medication and supervision from one of the top children's cardiologists in the nation. The expenses were enormous, even with insurance; a health catastrophe can clean out a bank account faster and deeper than most families can begin to replace.

That's one of the reasons it's important to accept our limitations, and be honest and open about our needs.

## Be Vulnerable

We were so overwhelmed by the avalanche of expenses, we had no recourse but to seek out help. It's one of the most difficult things for most men to do, recognizing the situation and admitting they need a hand. Yet a medical emergency is well-known as an unavoidable blow, and there are all kinds of foundations and programs available to help.

The expression of vulnerability is uncomfortable for men, and it can cause stress in their relationships as well as pushing away needed assistance. The wife may feel that her family's provision and security is threatened by her husband's pride; the husband may feel that admitting he needs help will un-man him as a confession of failure.

The Word of God, though, tells us that we should *bear one another's burdens, and so fulfill the law of Christ.*[5] If we don't share our burdens with the brethren, we're denying them an opportunity to fulfill that command. It's hard to say, "I need help," but the rewards are great. We have been amazed to see the love of Christ through the love of His people.

The Scriptures also say that the comfort we receive from God is sent *that we may be able to comfort those who are in any trouble, with the comfort with which we ourselves are comforted by God.*[6] When we draw back from accepting that blessing

---

[5] Galatians 6:2
[6] 2 Corinthians 1:4

which our friends and brethren extend, we are short-circuiting part of God's training.

We learned this from our experience with Katie's hospitalization. A friend of ours had a premature baby who spent several weeks in the neo-natal ICU. We wanted to help somehow, and we took them a few meals, but didn't know what more we could do. A few years later, after we'd lived in the hospital for a while ourselves, this same child came down with leukemia. Oh, were we ever prepared to help out this time! We knew the family needed meals taken to their home, sure, but they'd also need sustenance for the parents at the hospital. They needed snacks with protein and restaurant gift cards. They needed good, entertaining books to calm their frazzled nerves. They needed someone to help with errands and child care at the house and maybe a tank of gas for their van.

In short, we had learned something of the needs of an anxious parent stuck at a hospital out of town. We remembered the blessing of thoughtful friends who did the things which weren't obvious and traditional, but were very real needs a friend could address. We had been comforted, and we turned that experience around to comfort other families.

Even our children learn through the experience of trials. One year Hal was laid off from his job while Melanie was in bed with another high-risk pregnancy. One weekend a friend from church called and asked, "Are you going to be driving the van to church tomorrow?" Puzzled, Hal told him he would. The next day, he was surprised by a pounding.

Here in the South, the term "pounding" isn't a beating; it's an old word for a church event bringing food and gifts for a member of the congregation. It might be a welcome to a young new pastor, or a housewarming for a newlywed couple, or it may be the church's rallying behind a family in need.

When Hal and the children returned home, the kids burst into the house shouting, "Mama! Mama! Wait 'til you see what the church folks did!" They carried in load after load until the kitchen table—all seven feet of it—was loaded a yard deep with dry goods and cans, and the floor was covered with fishing coolers full of perishables and frozen food.

Hal gathered the children around and said, "I want you to remember this your whole life. There will be times when you'll think that you can't support your family. I want you to remember the Word says, '*I have not seen the righteous forsaken, Nor his descendents begging bread.*'[7] Usually, the Lord will provide what you need through your hard work, but sometimes He does it through the love of the brethren."

Months later, Hal was working again, the baby had been safely born and we were getting back to normal. One afternoon, the children were at chorus practice and the leader asked if anyone had any prayer requests before they opened the rehearsal in prayer. One little boy shyly and tearfully stood up and said, "My daddy lost his job and I don't know what in the world we're going to do!" A couple of our children immediately stood up and started sharing what God had done to take care of us: "...and He'll take care of your family, too." Melanie felt like crying tears of joy that our children had learned that life-changing lesson so young.

No one wants to go through trials, but when we share the burden with the brethren—and with our children—trials are often made more bearable and even a reason for rejoicing.

---

[7] Psalm 37:25

## Simplify at Home

No matter who is out of commission, it will impact the management of your household. You may have dreamed of your home gracing the cover of *Town & Country* or *Architectural Digest*, but when your living room has been converted to a sick room or your beloved is away at the hospital and your time is split between visiting your mate or running *all* the errands and doing *all* the chores in their absence, that dream has to be parked for a while. Anything which reduces the burden of maintaining the home ought to be considered.

We're firm proponents of using disposables when we're under stress. Melanie loves dishes and china, and she lays a beautiful table at holidays, but when sickness and other stresses get the upper hand, paper plates and plastic tableware reduce the cleanup task immensely (remember, we're a family of seven, even with three off at work or college). When our newborn went to ICU, our homeschool support group organized a paper drive—plates, cups, napkins, the works. It took dishwashing almost completely out of the way, and what a stress reliever that was!

This is one of those times to relax any high standards of housekeeping, too. The apostle Paul suffered from an unspecified ailment which he called *a thorn in the flesh*; he was convinced it was God's messenger to keep him humble.[8] Melanie's may be the housework; she believes the Lord lets this happen to teach us humility and compassion, too. She remembers when we had just one or two children, visiting the homes of friends with large families, and privately thinking, "Ugh." Now we've had eight children and several health episodes which left our home in more disarray than we ever saw theirs, and Melanie has prayed over and over that her

---

[8] 2 Corinthians 12:6-9

friends today would be more compassionate toward us than we may have been toward others in the past.

"Nowadays, I feel honored to be invited to a friend's house when it's a wreck," she tells people. "I know that means she trusts me not to be a jerk!"

A time of sickness may be a time to outsource some things, too. We've had teenagers from other families come in to help with cleaning, or accepted a friend's offer to do a few loads of laundry for us. Occasionally we've taken the whole backlog of laundry to a Laundromat and run it through industrial-style to catch up. It's survival time, and it's best to spend what little time you have on the things that are eternally important.

## Affection

When there's sickness in the house, physical affection may be the last thing on your mind. On the other hand, it might have moved up in your mate's priorities.

During some illnesses, relations might be curtailed; a mate might be in the hospital or restricted on doctor's orders, or simply too sick to be involved. It's still important to remember to show some physical affection—a touch, a kiss, a hug. The sick one may need reassurance and comfort in the expression of love. It's hard when you fear you're becoming a burden to those around you, when you wonder if your family and mate are beginning to resent you. You may be feeling ugly and unattractive (even a token effort to spruce up a bit can help, even if you can't leave the bed). You may need to be reminded you have a lover!

On the other hand, the well mate hasn't suddenly lost their sexual desires. Anxiety or stress from the other's illness may dampen their ardor somewhat, but they may need as much affection as their incapacitated mate can manage to express. Remember that our physical union is not solely for moments of romance and passion—there is a practical, comforting, and protective aspect to it as well.

From either side, the matter will involve some dying to self. The culture tells us that our sexual drives are irresistible and satisfying them is a matter of survival. The Bible says otherwise, if nowhere else than the requirement for the unmarried to remain celibate. If necessary, those who are married but somehow prevented can restrain themselves, too. Yet Paul encourages us not to deprive one another for long; that's where the other sacrifice comes in—being as affectionate and available as possible when you are feeling bad yourself. If both partners are trying their best to place the other's needs more highly than their own, they should be able to find a balance in the middle.

## Remembering Words

We often underestimate the power of our words, though the book of Proverbs is full of warnings about our patterns of speech and Jesus said *"by your words you will be justified, and by your words you will be condemned."* [9]

When Hal worked for the local power company, one of the most important lessons they taught was the danger of "error likely situations"—times when inclement weather, time pressures, fatigue, illness, or a dozen other things, put you off your game. They drilled into employees that when you found these distractions and burdens in your work situation, it was time to slow down, move with caution, and watch out for

---

9 Matthew 12:37

one another. When you're working in an electrical substation, a false move or an incorrect switch action can put a town in the dark...or a co-worker in the morgue.

Being sick is one of the strongest "error likely situations" we encounter in our marriages. The sick one is out of sorts, the unsick one is worried or overworked, and it is very easy to lose our temper or patience with one another. Usually it shows up in our words first.

Like Hal in the substation, it's time to watch our step and speak with extra care to be gentle, respectful of one another, and forgiving. We have to remember to speak to one another in love; otherwise, we begin seeing our mate as nothing but a team member carrying—or creating—a huge burden.

Hal's family was affectionate like Melanie's but tended to be more reserved. When we were engaged, he was surprised to learn how often Melanie wanted to hear him say, "I love you," even if he'd already said it several times that day. When we're dealing with sickness, we need to say it and hear it all the more frequently. We need the encouragement. It's not easy to be on either side of the sickbed quilt.

## Everyone on the Same Team

One of our friends with several children had lost a baby in a late term miscarriage, so when she conceived again a year or two later, she and her husband quietly agreed to hold off on the announcement until they could see if the pregnancy was off to a good start.

After several weeks, one of their children, friends of ours, came up to Melanie and quietly asked, "Would you please pray for my mother? I think she's really sick." This was news to Melanie, and she made some private inquiries about our friend's health. No, nothing out of the ordinary, was the answer she heard from several who knew her.

Finally she spoke with the mother herself, and the truth came out—our friend wasn't sick, just expecting. And then the parents realized what was happening: rather than protecting their children from anxiety and possible grief, they had frightened them with something worse. After all, the children reasoned, if Daddy is taking Mama off to the doctor again and again, and they won't tell us about it, something *awful* must be wrong. Really, *really* awful. And the children were worried sick.

We don't want to overburden our children's young shoulders, but they are more perceptive than we ever seem to realize. If they know that something is out of kilter but no information is coming, the scenerios and theories they concoct from their limited experience and understanding may be much worse than the truth.

When our youngest daughter was three, we took the family on a long driving trip to Manitoba. Occasionally she would wake up her car seat, and we would hear her quavering voice call forward, "*Where* are *we?*" It was largely new territory to us too, so we'd call back as truthfully as we knew, "Wisconsin," or "North Dakota." She'd answer back, "O-*kay...*" and doze off again. Was Wisconsin a comfort to her? No, she had no connections with the state. It was enough that *someone* knew where we were, and she trusted her parents could manage from there.

Children tend to be that way, particularly if they're young. If they see that Mom and Dad are aware of the problem and seem to have a plan to deal with it, they're content. If we confront sickness and injury with faith in God and trust in His care, then they will tend to follow suit. There's a reason Jesus pointed to the faith of children.

Older children can be a tremendous blessing. Teenagers can run errands, help with the housekeeping, mind the younger siblings, and generally help bear the parents' burdens. Our culture has a tendency to push adult expectations into the twenties or beyond; yet "It is *good for a man to bear the yoke in his youth*," the prophet Jeremiah wrote.[10] Historically, there's no reason we can't expect more of our young adults when we really need them. These times of working through family trial may be just what our young men and young women need to help them mature out of the adolescent mindset.

As we've weathered our storms, we noticed another pattern. While the younger children just want to be secure and the older siblings have adult roles to assume, the ones the middle are often frustrated and adrift. The ones just prior to their teenage years are old enough to understand the seriousness of a situation, but often they're overlooked and seldom called upon to help.

Ours have responded with almost gratitude when we found something useful for them to do. Melanie was down with another crisis pregnancy when the time came to file extensive financial aid documentation for one of our sons in college. Desperate for help, she grabbed our 12-year-old son and said, "Do you think you can run the scanner?"

"I never have, but I can try," he said.

He was the only one available, so Melanie shoved the huge stack of forms into his hands and talked him through the

---

[10] Lamentations 3:27

process. To her relief, he quickly found his way through the controls and successfully copied the paperwork, and he was delighted to be able to do something to really lift a burden from his bedridden Mom.

Whatever you do, don't try to hide things from each other. Our original train wreck of a pregnancy, the ten-weeks-head-down trying to save the life of our second son, was burden enough. Melanie was startled—and saddened—to discover afterward that through most of those months, Hal's job had been at risk due to a downsizing move at his employer, and he had kept it from her to prevent the additional stress from further impacting her and the baby's health. He was trying to protect them both, but on retrospect, Melanie was sorry she hadn't been able to spend some of that "rest" time praying for Hal's time of testing and anxiety at work. In the balance, usually it's just best to be straightforward with one another. You need each other, and a burden shared is a burden divided.

## Watch Out for the Aftershock

Our newborn daughter was seven weeks old, and had spent more than half her young life in the perinatal intensive care unit an hour from home. Hal had spent more time at the hospital than at home, and Melanie had hardly left the baby's bedside for four weeks. She was a rock, steady, engaging all the specialists and nurses with intelligent questions and standing by to comfort the tiny infant during procedures. At last, the cardiologists had hit on a drug which would control her racing heartbeat and—with God's blessing—keep her out of immediate, moment-by-moment danger. We were released, and left the hospital like any couple with a newborn... albeit an older one than most.

About ten minutes down the highway Melanie fell apart, weeping. Hal scanned from the road to his near-hysterical wife, back and forth.

"Sugar, are you okay?" he asked.

"I'll be fine," she sobbed.

In a few minutes the storm was over and Melanie grew calm again. We laughed about it later, and we were thankful none of the children but the sleeping baby were with us, but it was a prime example of a known fact. Often while the crisis is near, a couple can lace up their emotions tight and focus on surviving the emergency. When the calamity is over, for good or ill conclusion, it's not uncommon for everyone to simply collapse.

Hal's grandmother was a resident manager at a resort hotel. In her office was a wooden plaque which read, "As soon as the rush is over, I'm going to have a nervous breakdown. I worked for it, I owe it to myself, and nobody is going to deprive me of it."

Unfortunately, we can slip into that very mentality when going through a family emergency. It may be that we're not prepared to deal with the after effects of the trial. When we're under the load, we know that if we buckle, we may not be able to stand again. When the load lifts, we may drop the reins on our emotions and let fly with the accumulated stress and pain. We've held everything in for so long, when we relax our hold, the words which flow may be bitter, cross, or outrageous in a dozen ways.

If we know this is coming, we can warn the whole family to guard their tongues and their hearts until we all can transition back to a normal state. Spend more time in the Word, pray together, take extra care of one another's feelings. When the stress is fully relieved, you'll find your family strengthened and drawn closer. Like soldiers who have gone through the storm of combat together, you'll be a band of brothers!

## The Good Side of The Trials

It's hard to believe, but we have seen many benefits from the various trials which came to visit our family. We learned to trust God more deeply and fully; the hymn which sings *Jesus, Jesus—how I trust Him! How I've proved Him o'er and o'er!* [11] is like the story of our life. Our children have seen our faith tested and learned how believers cope with trials. We've learned to praise God in trials and blessings, too.

The fact is, trials and sickness are one more class in God's school for His people. Who has ever heard someone testify, "Things are fine and dandy for me, and I am really growing in the Lord!"? It's when we come to the end of our strength and have tapped out our resources that we can say with Paul, God's grace is sufficient for us, because His power is perfected in our weakness. *Therefore most gladly I would rather boast in my infirmities, that the power of Christ may rest upon me.* [12] And with His hand guiding, our marriage will emerge stronger than ever, refined in the fire, pure gold.

---

[11] Louisa M. R. Stead, "'Tis So Sweet To Trust In Jesus," 1882.
[12] 2 Corinthians 12:9

# ~ 4 ~

# On Submission

Be *kindly affectionate to one another with brotherly love, in honor giving preference to one another.*
— Romans 12:10

Melanie is a born leader. She typically looks around, assesses the situation, and cheerfully takes charge. To her, the whole idea of submission seemed like the most challenging part of marriage. She was raised in the days of "Anything you can do, I can do better!" and although she acknowledged that Scripture taught submission, it looked like it was going to be really, really hard. So she went into marriage determined to do what was right. She consulted Hal on every decision.

"What kind of bath mat do you like, honey?" she'd ask. Well, Hal really didn't care, but he tried to look interested, *"Are there different kinds of bathmats?"* he'd think.. He'd try hard to care; he'd work up an opinion and share it—though often it was only a frustration to Melanie, who *did* care about things like bath mats.

"What do you think of these lamps?" she asked him at the department store in the mall. "Do you like the ginger jar better than the wrought iron?" Hal, a pragmatic engineer-type, looked bemused. To him, a lamp was a fixture to hold a light bulb and illuminate a room. Once it was plugged in and working, it became invisible to him. *Does being a good husband require me to develop tastes in housewares?* he wondered.

It took a while for Melanie to realize that submitting to Hal meant something different than refusing to make a decision alone. She really thought that was what she was supposed to do—hard as it was. It was only after Hal gently and lovingly explained to her that he would really rather *not* be bothered about the kind of lamps we have, the color of the drapes, or even the bathmats, that she understood that there was more to submission than this.

We began to talk about this aspect of our brand new marriage and how we would carry out the Biblical prescription. Two things about submission began to dawn on us. First, it's about the mission, and second, the buck's got to stop somewhere.

## The Foundation of Biblical Submission

The concept of the husband's leadership is another universal principle rooted in the very creation of things. Why did God create Woman?

> Then the LORD God took the man and put him in the garden of Eden to tend and keep it. ...And the LORD God said, "It is *not good that man should be alone; I will make him a helper comparable to him.*"[1]

In the first days of the world, God gave Adam a mission, then created Eve to be his assistant. He instituted things that way. He also gave Eve certain characteristics and strengths that Adam did not have, so the one would complement the

[1] Genesis 2:15, 18

other. Eve's gifts and nature filled in the gaps in Adam's, and the opposite is true as well.

That told us that Melanie inherited the same role from her ancestor Eve—to be the helper God gave her husband. She would be his associate, assistant, and companion. She would manage things under his authority so that he could focus his strengths in areas he was uniquely gifted and responsible for. Hal would be better equipped to accomplish his mission because of the supporting role played by Melanie.

And to Hal, it was perfectly acceptable for her to choose the bathmats and the lamps—in fact, it was actually best, because allowing her to manage the houseware choices freed him up to do what *he* needed to do. She could freely use her talents to bless our young family because that allowed Hal to do his job better. Now, if Hal had wanted the responsibility for the bathmats, or had deeply held opinions about table lamps, it would have been wrong for her to take care of it without further consultation, but he didn't. He needed a wife, not a robot!

The second part is God's assignment of responsibility. Democracy stumbles when there are only two equally-powered voting members. How do you break a tie? Egalitarian theories of relationship sound nice when everyone is in general agreement, but what happens when they inevitably have a different of opinion? There are no tie-breakers.

We didn't start marriage with plans to disagree, and honestly, we seldom do even today. When a difference arises, though, somebody's got to have the deciding vote or we'll just stand still pulling in different directions. That role has been given to Hal, the husband. Sometimes that's hard for Melanie the wife to accept. Some years ago Hal's employer undertook a major restructuring move, and Hal was notified that his position was being eliminated. In a few months, he would be laid off. We were frightened; we'd only moved to that job and purchased that house a year and a half before, and it seemed completely overwhelming. After several weeks of looking and interviewing, Hal had two job offers. The first was on the beautiful, moss-draped Sea Islands of Georgia, a lovely and romantic spot which had always captured Melanie's imagination. Surrounded by history and coastal scenery, Hal would join a profitable company at a higher salary and good career prospects at hand.

The second offer was quite different. The pay was acceptable, in an odd subset industry related to the one he was leaving. The town was in the dusty sandhills of eastern North Carolina, a location enlived by the unending roar of trucks along I-95 and an annual celebration called "Mule Days."

More money among the live oaks of the Georgia coast, or a lateral career move to an unremarkable town known for its farm animals. *That* decision was obvious, thought Melanie.

Imagine her surprise when Hal came to her and said, "I have really prayed about this decision, and I've decided we need to take the job here, in North Carolina." Shock! Dismay! "How could he think that? I can't understand it!" Melanie thought to herself.

And then she did what she knew she had to. She told Hal what *she* thought was the right decision and why, but assured him that no matter what he decided, she would cheerfully support him and not throw it back at him later. Well, he stuck to that decision and she so did she. We moved just a couple of hours down the road and she kept her mouth shut. What's really interesting is that now, fourteen years later, that move was very *clearly* providential. We don't believe we'd be writing this book except for the chain of circumstances that God began with that move to the "wrong job" in the "wrong town." Hal's decision to stay in the state we were in allowed us to stay involved in state homeschool leadership, which led to opportunities for public speaking, which led to our writing, and which led to knowing the people who could help us get started. That "wrong" decision was absolutely the right one.

What's more, a few short years after we moved, the new company declared bankruptcy in the wake of 9/11 and as Melanie had feared, Hal was laid off again. At that point it would have been really easy for Melanie to throw that decision at him in frustration and anger, but she'd promised not to and she kept her word. In the light of what has happened since then, she's thankful she did, too, because she would have been embarrassingly wrong.

Submission is not bondage, but rather freedom to Melanie. It means that she doesn't have to worry and agonize that she's making the wrong decision, but it doesn't prevent her from making dozens of decisions every day about our family and our business. She just undertakes them in light of our agreed-upon mission, our shared principles. That's the way Hal likes it. And when the decision is critical, Hal has the final say, and Melanie can stop worrying. She's seen what God can do with "unwise" decisions and she's learned she's not omniscient—He is.

## What the Bible Says About Submission

When he wrote to the church in Corinth, Paul addressed problems he saw in a congregation where worship services threatened to break down in confusion as multiple members clamored to share their thoughts and talents in the meeting. Encouraging them to give each other a turn to speak, sing, and so on, Paul singled out one group—the women:

> *For God is not the author of confusion but of peace, as in all the churches of the saints. Let your women keep silent in the churches, for they are not permitted to speak; but they are to be be submissive, as the Law also says. And if they want to learn something, let them ask their own husbands at home; for it is shameful for women to speak in church.*[2]

In other places, he explains that God called men, not women, to lead His church. In the passages describing ordained church officers, Paul specifies that they are *men*, underscoring it in three different passages by requiring them to be *"husband of one wife."*[3] It's certainly true that Paul was speaking into a seriously broken culture, where many popular cults were ruled by priestesses or featured religious prostitution in their ceremonies. In that society, a woman in a prominent religious role was a hallmark of false religions; naturally, it was an issue right in front of the early church.

And yet Paul goes back to Genesis to argue a more universal case, pointing to the order of creation—*"For Adam was formed first, and then Eve"*—and the order of the Fall—for *"Adam was not deceived, but the woman was deceived and became a transgressor..."*[4]—to explain the reasons for this arrangement. And in Genesis chapter 3, the submission of the Woman to the Man was included in God's judgment on the fallen couple. Along with difficulty and pain in childbearing, a curse was pronounced on the woman's calling just as God cursed the

---

[2] 1 Corinthians 14:33-35
[3] 1 Timothy 3:2, 12 and Titus 1:6
[4] 1 Timothy 2:12-14

fields in which the man would labor, He concludes, *"Your desire* shall *be for your husband, And he shall rule over you."*[5]

## It's About the Mission

As we see it, submission isn't about repression or unworthiness or *machismo*, as the world would portray it. Rather, it's about accomplishing the mission. God is not whimsical, and He is sovereign. Every person and every couple on the earth has been placed by Him for a reason, a purpose, or a mission. Adam was given the mission to tend the garden, name the newly-created animals, and other tasks; Eve was created to be a helper in completing his mission. The two of them were given a mutual assignment to have children and raise a family, to populate and cultivate the earth, and to rule over the animal kingdom.[6] Frequently in our home we challenge our sons with the question, "What are you doing to advance the family mission?" It's meant to remind them their purpose in life is not their own pleasure but to serve others. There is a greater goal in view than their leisure time. There is a mature sort of joy and fulfillment which comes from pursuit of that path of loving service to others. And that is a foundational principle of submission—it's about the wife helping the husband advance the family mission.

That mission will be different for each family. Paul compared the church to a human body; he explained to the Corinthians that God gives different gifts to members of His church in order to fill different roles in His kingdom. We can't all be hands or eyes in the body of Christ, nor should we want to be.[7] Likewise, every couple is made up of two differently-gifted individuals, suited to each other, and to their shared mission.

---

[5] Genesis 3:16
[6] Genesis 1:28
[7] 1 Corinthians 12:4-28

That means submission in *your* home will be lived out differently than in your neighbor's. Melanie submits to Hal and blesses him by speaking in public, managing the finances for our family and business, teaching our children at home, and many other creative applications of her talents and gifts, Instead of looking at other families and asking, "Why aren't we more like them?"—or judgmentally, "Why aren't they more like us?"—we look to the missional opportunities which God has given to our family, and seek to accomplish those purposes...not someone else's.

## The Buck Stops Here

Whenever we watch a movie with our kids, we always try to discuss the underlying theme of the film. What's the message? Is there a clear statement of what the story is trying to teach us?

In the movie *Spider-Man*, the hero Peter Parker is told by his Uncle Ben, "Remember, with great power comes great responsibility."

Jesus told us the same thing: *"For everyone to whom much is given, from him much shall be required; and to whom much has been committed, of him they will ask the more."*[8]

This is the aspect of biblical submission that we modern folk don't like to talk about—the idea that God has granted the husband authority over the wife. He is expected to be in charge of his home. In fact, when Paul gives the qualifications of a bishop or overseer in the church, he expects that he's *one who rules his own house well... for if a man does not*

---

[8] Luke 12:48 (NKJV)

*know how to rule his own house, how will he take care of the*
*church of God?* 9

Some will be quick to point out that several translations
render the word "manage," and that would be correct. The
word in the original Greek means to preside over, to care
for, to be a protector or guardian. It means to be attentive
to a matter, as well. And these shades of meaning illustrate
an important truth—that the wife's submission is given to a
husband who is called not just to direct the family but take
responsibility for it.

And it's not a simple kind of responsibility. The passage
which says the wife should submit to the husband just like
the church submits to Jesus Christ—fully and willingly—also
says the husband which receives this sort of devotion is
expected to earn it:

> *...just as the church is subject to Christ, so let the*
> *wives be to their own husbands in every way. Hus-*
> *bands, love your wives, just as Christ also loved*
> *the church **and gave Himself for her...** 10*

In other words, wives are told to submit, but husbands
are told to *die*. At least, that's the measure of love Christ gave
to us in the church. There's no room for selfishness in any
degree, if your calling is service to the point of death.

This is the way the Word portrays leadership and it is very
different from the world's caricature of lording it over your
wife until she shows cowed subservience. We call this biblical
model "servant-leadership," and like we speak about elsewhere,
it's part of the way we define love—placing someone else's

---

9 1 Timothy 3:4-5
10 Ephesians 5:24-25, emphasis added.

concerns ahead of your own. If that kind of self-sacrificial love rules in your marriage, than tyranny isn't a problem.

Occasionally in our family one of the older children tries to assert authority over the younger, in a way which oversteps any temporary deputizing we might have done. We find it usually quells the attempt if we tell them, "We can give you authority over your little brother, but then we'll hold you responsible for whatever he does. Is that what you want?"

It's the classic captain-of-the-ship problem. The skipper has to answer for his crew; if they run amok somehow, certainly they bear their own guilt, but the officer in charge is responsible as well. Likewise, the husband may consider certain roles in the family to belong to his wife, and she may agree, but ultimately he's accountable for whether the family is fed, the laundry is done, the dishes washed, bills paid, and diapers changed. With this attitude, he can look on the beloved helper God has gifted to him, and understand that when she's doing "woman's work" it's a burden she's lifting off *him*.

## Biblical Submission

At the end of the matter, we have to remember there's a lot of submission in Scripture, and it's not just wifely. We are told to submit to God,[11] to the governing authorities,[12] and to our church leaders.[13] Children are commanded to obey their parents.[14] Christians are even told to submit to

---

[11] James 4:7
[12] Romans 13:1
[13] Hebrews 13:17
[14] Colossians 3:20

one another in the Lord.[15] And yes, wives should submit to their husbands[16]—*their own husbands*, the Word says.[17]

Women are not to submit to all husbands, or all men, but only to their own husbands and the authorities God has placed over them. This idea of women submitting to all men is not Biblically supported. In Scripture we see women in business and women in leadership outside of the church and home. It's hard enough to get those relationships right; let's not create additional burdens God did not give us the grace and wisdom, nor the commandment, to bear.

## False Submission

Anyone who has served in the military or another rigidly-enforced management structure has seen or experienced rebellion by outward obedience. A young lieutenant or a newly-graduated supervisor can be put in his place by the veterans under his authority, undermining the mission and leaving the boss exposed to trouble while making a show of strict, dumb obedience.

You don't have to join the army or sign up with a unionized mill to see this in action. Sometimes it happens right there in the family room.

Melanie remembers leaving a field trip with several friends and their children, and suggesting a stop for ice cream or a milkshake. One mother demurred, saying, "I'll need to call my husband."

---

[15] Ephesians 5:21
[16] Ephesians 5:22
[17] Paul. "Ephesians 5." *Biblos Interlinear Bible*. N.p., n.d. Web. 28 Aug. 2012. ‹http://interlinearbible.org/ephesians/5.htm›.

It sounds like a *reductio ad absurdum,* carrying an issue to the point of absurdity, but we meet wives like that. They go beyond asking their newlywed husband whether he likes fuzzy bath mats or smooth—instead, they ostentatiously ask their husbands to endorse every little thing and the simplest decisions. Sadly, many of them will speak disparaging and disrespectfully of their mate in the same breath.

"I'll need to check with my husband before I sign up for that field trip *and who knows when he'll decide!* He just procrastinates all the time. It's ridiculous and it's going to cost him one day."

Is this submission or not? Are God and Christ honored by outward show with inward rebellion? The answer is obvious. Once Melanie confronted a dear friend of hers who seemed to behave that way. Her friend explained that she knew she had a heart of rebellion toward her husband and that's *precisely* why she consulted him in every little thing. Perhaps spiritual self-discipline lies behind other cases like hers, but regardless, the attitude of the heart is once again, the heart of the whole matter.

Another kind of false submission is the supposed referral of a situation to the husband, taking a form of passive aggression.

We knew a couple who had agreed to homeschool and like most of these families, the wife would be the primary instructor and decision-maker about the teaching. At one point the wife became frustrated with their history curriculum and asked the husband if he would choose between several possibilities. Not surprisingly, he hadn't considered the matter in detail—after all, that task had been delegated, in his mind—and he had neither information nor much conviction about any of the alternative textbooks his wife suggested.

At that point, she withdrew from the discussion and left the whole thing on his plate. Whether he knew it or not, she decided to suspend any history instruction until she got orders from Headquarters. The communiqué never arrived, and so history was dead for the remainder of that year..."because my husband hasn't decided what curriculum we should use."

This was a failure on both their parts. She should have asked clearly, "Do you want to make this decision, or do you want me to take care of it?" Holding the family's activities hostage to try and wring an unwilling decision out of her husband was *not* submission nor was it very helpful to him.

On the other hand, he should have openly said, "Dear, you know I don't know nearly as much as you do about this. Please make this decision for us." It is *not* leadership to let things drop without resolution because it's easier than dealing with the issue.

## Leadership Struggles

Just as wives struggle with submission, husbands struggle with leadership. In some cases men will take their God-given authority and wield it capriciously over their wives and children. They make arbitrary decisions and issue directives to test their family's responsiveness. They speak down to their "subjects" and even enjoy degrading and humiliating them.

The resentment, anger, and rebellion it breeds can drive entire families away from the Gospel. We read scathingly hostile articles and blogs by the children of controlling homes. Sadly, we know some of the fathers (and mothers) of these homes, and not infrequently, they are well-intentioned and genuine followers of Christ. They truly thought that an iron hand on the reins would keep the family from straying into the errors and sin of the parents' past. The perception of tyranny in the eyes of the children was more felt than real, because layers and layers of relationship issues had grown up between them and their parents. Often the father had missed the "servant" part of leadership, the mother was not showing true respect to her husband, and the children grew up to despise the "hypocrisy" of both.

Neither wives nor children are animals or slaves. True, biblical submission and obedience must come from the heart. As leaders, we should not be making this harder for them by our own thoughtlessness or sinful behaviors.

But for other men, the temptation is to abdicate, to refuse to lead. Some men don't want the responsibility, others want to avoid conflict, but in either case they won't make decisions. This leaves their wives in a bad place: she either takes up the reins herself, or she watches the family run into a ditch.

We know of a couple whose very effective teaching ministry was forced to close down during an economic downturn. The husband sank into deep depression; he wouldn't participate in family decisions, he wouldn't work in the family business that remained after the closure, he wouldn't take his family to church. He was hurting, and he just quit. He wasn't intending to leave his family in the lurch, but they nearly lost their house before he began to recover.

Why didn't he get help? Because in his depression, he couldn't recognize his own symptoms. When their family doctor met with him, he was surprised to find the doctor concerned with *his* state of mind instead of his wife's. Guys in this shape need other men in their lives, friends or pastors, to hold them accountable and help them get through. If they have abandoned their position of leadership at home, it may be due to a treatable condition they can't yet identify.

Other men may be just passive by nature or may hate conflict. A husband might simply give up rather than face his wife's criticism again. Another may be so accommodating to his wife's wishes, he provokes stress in her by constantly deferring to her wishes and forcing *her* to make all the decisions. The best answer in either of these situations is to talk it out. Many times we have heard women complain that they *have* to take charge, and we wonder if their husbands realize their wives would rather *not* be in that position.

Eventually we all have to get out of comfortable patterns in order to become more Christ-like. Passive husbands may have to force themselves to step up to the plate. Forceful wives may need to step back and give their husbands room to lead.

## Liberty

How submission works out in your home is going to depend on you and your mate. One couple we know doesn't talk on the phone during the day because the interruptions annoy them both; another lives with their walkie-talkies in hand, discussing decisions and directions constantly hour by hour. Both couples are happy; both ways are acceptable. The point is the heart: does the husband have a heart of servant-leadership, seeking the best for his wife and family, instead of a heart of self-indulgence and tyranny? Does the wife have a heart of submission that seeks to help her husband in the way he wants, even if that means making decisions—or refraining from them? The attitude is what matters.

We have the liberty to express these things differently in each of our homes. We do not have the liberty to abandon the principles of Scripture and resort to sinful ways of dealing with one another.

The critical thing is that both of you remember that the husband bears the final authority. That can be a real comfort—or a serious warning. It's also important that both of you be comfortable with the balance. It's hard to believe, but many "bossy" wives would really be delighted to hand over the gavel if only their husbands would pick it up.

When we both embrace our God-given roles and the necessity for showing preference and love for the other, the wife's submission bears no resemblance to the world's caricatures, but when linked with her husband's sacrificial love, is one more way in which we portray Christ to those around us.

# ~ 5 ~

# Fidelity and Loyalty Are
# Not Mutual Funds

*His heart safely trusts in her...*

— Proverbs 31:11

*Husbands, love your wives, even as Christ loved
the church...*

— Ephesians 5:25

Hal was trained as an engineer. In our fathers' time, the plan was to choose a company soon after you left college, and then retire from that company forty years later. We didn't realize that for us the career would mean frequent job changes and relocations from coast to coast. When times get tough, we found, companies look for ways to cut corners, and in manufacturing, sometimes an engineering staff seems like an expensive luxury. Hal and many of his colleagues learned to keep their resumes up to date! As we moved from Mississippi to Florida to California to Louisiana to North Carolina—and a few times within state—Hal started to realize he was losing friends. Not that he did anything wrong, or they did anything wrong, but they simply lost track of one another. People that he went out to lunch with, people who worked on projects and committees with him, people he spoke with everyday—when we moved on, most of them simply disappeared.

That bothered Hal at first. Then he realized that there are friends, and then there are *friends*. There are people who share a common activity, like colleagues in the office or classmates in college, and as long as you are sharing that job or that activity, they might be real buddies—but the relationship didn't go any deeper. When we moved on, there wasn't much to call them back to mind.

But there are friends who are truly closer than a brother (which is easy in Hal's case, since he never had a brother growing up). These are people who have stood beside us in crisis, people we've stood beside when it was their life in a tailspin instead of ours, people we knew we could trust. These are the ones we still call, send Christmas cards to, sometimes visit, even if we're living hundreds or thousands of miles apart.

What's the difference? Hal once called his forgotten colleagues "friends." Our closest confidantes in college were "friends." We have several hundred people on Facebook who call us "friend." What's the difference?

Faithfulness and loyalty. You might say fidelity. They've been there when we needed them, and we'll be there for them when their own time comes. We can depend on them, and they can depend on us. We like each other deeply enough to make sacrifices for one another—with joy. We love each other because we've kept faith with each other, and we make a point to think the best of each other.

In the Song of Solomon, the bride says, *"This is my beloved, and this is my friend."*[1] Our marriage relationship is even closer than that—Jesus says that the husband and wife become one

---

[1] Song of Solomon 5:16

flesh.[2] Paul said that our marriage is meant to be a mirror of Jesus' love for his church.[3] It's powerful stuff. And this relationship needs to have that same sort of faithfulness, loyalty, dependability, trust—it requires fidelity. So let's talk about it.

## So, what are fidelity and loyalty?

Fidelity is faithfulness, keeping the faith, doing what is promised. Often it means keeping a commitment, and avoiding things that damage it. Often it means that certain things you *don't* do, for the sake of the thing.

We think "I'd never be unfaithful," and that certainly should be our intent, but faithfulness goes way beyond avoiding the farthest extreme of adultery. Faithfulness says, "I'll do you no harm." It's a heart attitude, an attitude of commitment to the relationship and to the person. It's the essence of "'til death do us part." Fidelity is obedience to your oaths.

In an age when the divorce rate among Christians is no different from that of unbelievers, to the shame of the church, we seem to have forgotten what an oath is. One weekend we had the privilege of seeing what it meant to an older generation to promise "For better or for worse."

The marriage of Melanie's maternal grandparents is not a happily-ever-after story. Her grandfather was an extremely difficult man to live with in his youth—a wild and angry man. After he repented and settled down, her grandmother suffered repeated bouts with cancer and several major surgeries. In spite of their challenges, they did their duty toward one another and did not abandon the marriage. They paid their vows—for themselves, for the Lord, and for their family. They

---

[2] Matthew 19:5-6
[3] Ephesians 5:25-32

have lost almost all of their many siblings to death, helped a daughter through becoming a young widow, and loved and shepherded us all through heartbreaks, health breakdowns and job losses.

Then in their eighties, Melanie's grandfather developed Alzheimers' and his health declined to the point that he needed constant help.

Nana kept him at home as long as she could, but she was unable to pick him up when he kept falling down. When we visited, he was undergoing rehab at a nursing home. Even in old age, the wife of his youth had not abandoned him; every day she drove back and forth to the nursing home to feed him, take him to the bathroom so he didn't lose his dignity, and bring him treats and happiness. It was a lovely sight to see her tender devotion to a man who no one would have once faulted her for running from. To see his once strong arms reach in trust and need to his wife, "Are you coming back soon?" To see her save him a piece of cake, saying, "I'll take this to Ray later. He always loved red velvet cake." To see him cared for and clean and well-fed when so many were so lonely.

When Melanie told Nana what a blessing this was for her, she told us how he had taken her from doctor to doctor and hospital to hospital when she had cancer, how he'd cared for her when she couldn't. We thought of Ecclesiastes:

> *Two* are *better than one,*
> *Because they have a good reward for their labor.*
> *For if they fall, one will lift up his companion.*
> *But woe to him* who is *alone when he falls,*
> *For* he has *no one to help him up.*
> *Again, if two lie down together, they will keep warm;*

*But how can one be warm alone?*
*Though one may be overpowered by an-*
*    other, two can withstand him.*
*And a threefold cord is not quickly broken.*[4]

This is Christian marriage. We are called to be a living picture of the eternal love between Christ and the church. Does it seem impossible to you? How can you love and sacrifice through all the hurt and hard times of this fallen world? We would recommend you see that your marriage is of three strands: the two of you and He is who is able to make *us able* to keep our vows.

Since that visit several years ago, Papa Ray has gone home to be with his Savior. Hal and the boys gloriously sang, "When The Roll Is Called Up Yonder" at his funeral. He so loved to hear us sing! Even after Alzheimers had taken all his memory, when we would begin to sing, his voice would join in, the words flowing directly from the heart. Nana misses him terribly, but one day we will all be reunited and her faithfulness will be rewarded. That is fidelity.

Loyalty is similar but involves the feelings of faithfulness that go beyond obedience to your vow, but choose to do more.

Loyalty says, "I'll do positive good," and "I will happily be faithful to you!" It's loyalty that makes a big brother who just called his little brother a nerd, turn and whack his friend who agrees. "He's my brother and *you* won't call him names!"[5] It's loyalty that made the little girl who fled a war torn area carrying her little brother shrug off the praise of others, "He's not heavy, he's my brother!" Faithfulness gives peace and security, loyalty gives joy.

---

[4] Ecclesiastes 4:9-12
[5] It would be better if the brother didn't call him names, either.

There are all kinds of fidelity and loyalty and we find occasions every day to practice these virtues or to deny them.

## Fidelity of the body

Fidelity of the body is obvious. *"Thou shalt not commit adultery."* Uncompromising commandment, that.

There is no excuse, not ever, for adultery. In the traditional marriage vows we commit ourselves to "forsaking all others." Lack of communication, falling out of love, thoughts that you married the wrong person, believing he or she doesn't treat you right, or lack of physical intimacy are all excuses just trying to justify sin.

Here's the thing: our culture promises us that *we* are the most important consideration in our life. We have friends who have teetered on the edge of divorce, or who actually did divorce, and even Christians say to them, "You need to do what you need to do to be happy," and "It's time to move on and find somebody that loves you." Is that Biblical? It is not.

Where in Scripture does it say, "You can break the law of God if it makes you happier"? Where does it say, "Your purpose on earth is to seek your own pleasure. Do whatever you need to do to be happy!"? Does the Word of God tell you to stay in a marriage only when you feel you're in love?

That last question is critical. The Bible does not say "Check to see if you still love her," or "Feel around and see if there's any bubbling affection for him any more." No, it commands you to love. *"Husbands, love your wives."* [6] Older women are told to teach the younger women *to love their husbands* [7]

---

[6] Ephesians 5:25, Colossians 3:19
[7] Titus 2:4

Love for our mate is a command, and something which can be taught and learned. It's not a rush of feeling, but rather, a conscious choice of action and thought. In fact, that should be a source of hope for us—we can be loving even when we don't feel especially affectionate.

No one wakes up one morning and says, out of the blue, "I think I'll destroy my marriage today. Why don't I commit adultery?" The strength or weakness of a marriage starts long before that. Our habits of thought and decision lay the groundwork for the path we take when temptations arise.

## Fidelity of the eyes

The Bible tells us to be filled up with the beauty of our own wives, and not to be window shopping around. Job said, "*I have made a covenant with my eyes—why should I look on a maiden?*" [8] Proverbs warns about seductive women, and says "*do not lust after her beauty in your heart, nor let her allure you with her eyelids.*" [9] Jesus, of course, said that looking at a woman in order to lust after her is adultery of the heart—even if the physical act is never carried out.[10]

We offer a workshop session called "Shining Armor: Your Son's Battle for Purity." It's always packed, and afterward folks line up to talk to us. At least half of the women ask, "How can I teach my son purity when his father has wandering eyes?" Just in case you think your mate doesn't know—they do! And so do your children. And so does your God.

This has become a lot harder a sin to resist because of the ubiquitous nature of the Internet and the incredible lie

---

[8] Job 31:1
[9] Proverbs 6:25
[10] Matthew 5:28

that no one will ever know. We recently heard of a Christian husband and father who became involved in Internet pornography. Before long, he'd fallen into perverse and highly illegal pornography. One day, he came to his senses, repented of this sin, and confessed to his wife and pastor. He wiped his hard drive and put himself under accountability. From all evidence, it seemed that God had restored this man to the right path and had freed him from this sin. Understandably, he thought all was behind him.

Then one day there was a knock at the door. A federal investigator was there with a warrant to confiscate his computer; an investigation into a child pornography ring had uncovered this man's connection as a customer. Technicians easily recovered the files from the re-formatted disc, and the man was convicted and sent to prison. Don't believe the lie that no one will ever know.

God takes this seriously. We need to as well.

We're in a highly sexualized culture. So were ancient Greece and ancient Rome. When the New Testament speaks about it, the writers were sitting in a culture very much like our own. We don't have an excuse because it's hard to avoid.

We have to recognize that wandering eyes and wandering thoughts are a danger to our own souls and a threat to our marriage. We need to take some serious positive steps and train ourselves not to swim in that cultural stream.

This fidelity of the eyes also applies to non-sexual things. While men are commanded to love their wives, wives are commanded to respect their husbands.[11] It can be very tempting to compare your husband to men that are more advanced,

_____
[11] Ephesians 5:33

more godly, better leaders, better providers, whatever, just as men can be tempted to compare their wives to women who are more attractive or younger or more understanding.

Both kinds of wandering looks are dangerous. God gave you the right mate for you. Comparing your mate to others just makes you discontented. And we're going to share with you a very important secret:

## You get the mate you believe in

If a lady believes her husband is on his way to becoming a great man, he will be. If she has confidence in him, he'll have confidence in himself. If she respects him, he'll have self-respect. If she believes in him, he will do everything in his power to live up to her expectations. If he is struggling in his job or stumbling repeated over a besetting sin in his life, a wife who constantly points out his failures and short-comings will probably succeed only in depressing his efforts to overcome them.

On the other hand, if a man believes his wife is beautiful, she'll feel beautiful herself, be much more affectionate and strive to please him. A loving—and wise—husband knows that his wife is more than aware of any criticism he might offer.[12] A lot of ice cream and brownies have given their lives in the cause of cheering women up! Instead, the man that makes his wife feel beautiful gives her the encouragement she needs to put on perfume, to dress up, to wear jewelry, to welcome his advances—to make her own!

---

12  We've never understood folks that tell you you're fat. "Really? My word! I hadn't noticed! How in the world did I buy all these giant clothes and not have any idea I'd gained weight? Why, *thank you* for letting me know. I'll go get gastric band surgery tomorrow! I'd have never known without you!"

## Fidelity of the mind and heart

The mind is where fidelity hits the road. Sometimes we are faithful and loyal completely in the physical realm, but have a constant stream of infidelity running through our minds—whether it is constant criticism or sexual fantasy, infidelity of the mind is very tempting. Like the Internet, Satan promises no one will ever know, but it's not true.

Stress reveals who we really are. *"For from within, out of the heart of men, proceed evil thoughts, adulteries, fornications, murders..."* [13]

When things are going great, we can fake it, we can behave well and keep our thoughts to ourselves. In the refiner's fire of stress, our true feelings come out. That's why we have to make sure we are true blue all the way down.

But how can we do that? Here's a clue: Emotions are not reliable. *"The heart is deceitful above all things... who can know it?"* [14] the prophet Jeremiah asked. So, given that we are commanded to be faithful, commanded to love, commanded to respect, these are things we can *do* and the feelings come later. Fidelity of the heart—faithful all the way down.

## Avoiding traps—confiding in others

There are traps all around us, and we easily stumble if we don't take the heart and mind issues seriously enough. For example, Proverbs 31 says of the godly woman and her husband, *"His heart safely trusts in her."* [15] You should never

---

[13] Mark 7:21
[14] Jeremiah 17:9
[15] Proverbs 31:11a

say anything behind your mate's back that you would not say in front of them—it's a trust issue.

Women talk to each other about personal issues in a way that men find cold-blooded. At a campground stop recently, Melanie came back from the bath house after stopping by another family's site for less than five minutes. One of our sons came to Hal aghast; how did Mom know all about this other family's hometown, their job situation, relocation plans, the names and ages of their children, their educational arrangements, and a bit of the husband's family history? Hal explained that women naturally share all kinds of information when they first meet—"They're like our intelligence wing," he said with a smile.

Although seeking the advice of an older and wiser woman can be a tremendous help, wives need to be careful about prayer requests that expose their husbands in a way they would not appreciate. Don't confide in those who will encourage you in your own sin, taking your side in a dispute when you need to be held to account instead. Seek out those who speak the truth in love! For men, the risk may be in confiding in their mothers, who will naturally be on their side. As the mother of six sons, Melanie has to recognize that one day our boys will need to replace her as their confidant and turn to their wives. We have a friend whose husband can't seem to put his wife and children above his mother's desires and unfortunately, the mother was against them ever marrying. She has done everything in her power to tear their marriage apart.

Another friend is the mother in the equation. For all the right reasons, she and her husband were against their son marrying, but once he was married, instead of trying to stay involved in their lives and be a witness, she refused to have any contact with them until he repented. Unfortunately, her definition of repentance was very demanding: that he would admit he was wrong, move back close to them, go their church again, and more. It was a whole list of things that would basically remove all his autonomy as the head of his own family. She was trying to force him to choose between disloyalty to his wife and losing his whole very close family. This is not a righteous thing! As dear and well-meaning as our friends are, their son would be foolish at that point to confide in them. Since then, they realized that rather than continuing to take a stand that "this wasn't our idea" they would have much more influence by being involved with their lives.

## Emotional infidelity

Closely related to confiding in the wrong person is the danger of emotional infidelity. It is very tempting online: "There is no danger. After all, he lives across the country." It starts as just friendly chatting, then a little confidence is exchanged. The other person is on your side—shoring you up, feeling sorry for you. Before long they seem to be all you've ever dreamed of. The reality is that you only see a fantasy—a carefully edited view of reality. You can't smell their body odor and you don't have to pick up their sweat socks. He snaps at his wife when he's tired, but not at you. It is a fantasy!

Does that happen to serious Christians? Yes—it has brought down more than one ministry. A pastor or teacher or author with struggles in their marriage discovers a friend online and forms a relationship. Confidences begin to be exchanged, and when travel for ministry or study gives an opportunity, friendship becomes something much, much more. Reputations are easily wrecked and painful to rebuild, and marriages more so. We have to avoid the very first step—giving our emotions and trust to someone outside of our mate.

## The appearance of evil

Paul wrote to the church at Thessalonika to *Abstain from all appearance of evil.*[16] If we keep ourselves out of situations which *look* evil, we may avoid placing ourselves into circumstances which facilitate actual sin.

A pastor of our acquaintance was a devoted father and deeply in love with his wife. He had a gift for counseling, and because he had never been tempted to stray from his marriage, he thought nothing about counseling women who needed Godly advice one-on-one.

Eventually he began advising a woman who seemed to need more and more counseling. People began to talk—why *was* she so often in his office? Why did she call for him so frequently? When he was accused of having an affair, his wife asked him—and he was hurt and angry, no one believed he was innocent. Up to that point, he *was* innocent, but as he saw his reputation questioned, the only person who seemed to have faith in him was the woman he was counseling (Note the power of that!). Soon he was in her arms. His marriage came to an end, he lost his long-held position in a large church, and he remarried the woman he had joined in adultery.

Because he was incautious about being alone with a member of the opposite sex (not to mention placing himself in a role of concern and support for her), he was falsely accused of unfaithfulness. His pride then opened the door to temptation, and he walked through. It might have all been avoided

---

[16] 1 Thessalonians 5:22.

if he had counseled the woman with another person present, or at the least, with the office door open. Now he pastors another congregation in the same town where his first wife and children live, and they re-live the betrayal every time they pass the church. What a tragedy—and how avoidable.

## The false promise of privacy

Ironically, one aspect of modern relationships has offered us the option to completely conceal ourselves in the name of "friendship." The rise of social media like Facebook and Twitter has made it much easier to get yourself in trouble, and at the same time the Internet has made the enticing promise that "no one will ever know."

As our children have reached their teens, we have allowed them to join in with certain social media. We have to explain to them very carefully that not everyone you meet online is what they claim to be. Every parent has heard of pedophiles stalking the chat rooms to see if they can lure a young girl or boy to a face-to-face meeting. The same things happen to grown-ups. Divorce lawyers are finding gold in the Facebook accounts of straying husbands and wives who found an old friend from high school or college after so many years, and the natural conversation to "catch up" went from jobs and number of children to more intimate matters.

## You can't really delete

We warn our children that information posted online goes out of the control of the originator. They are amazed to learn that message traffic on the Internet and cell phone chats may be archived several times between the sender and the recipient. Recently we had an illustration of how persistent that data is. Hal accidentally destroyed a number of critical emails in his business account while clearing out old correspondence. Because he was trying to reclaim storage space, he went the full step of deleting then actually purging the data from his web server. Yet when he discovered the error, it was only a matter of a few emails to tech support to recover every message he had deleted for the previous month. It only *looked* like it was gone, when really it was safely backed up in the service provider's archives.

In the past year, we've seen numerous public figures torpedoed by incautious messages on Twitter or even person-to-person SMS chats on cell phones. In some cases, public spokesmen for state agencies found their careers cut off; in others, high-profile job offers were withdrawn from young aspirants whose Facebook or blog comments came to light. When the scandal involved elected officials and celebrities, the entire world was invited to the spectacle.

You don't have to wait for the end of time to experience what the Word of God warns about:

> *Nothing is covered up that will not be revealed, or hidden that will not be known. Therefore whatever you have said in the dark shall be heard in the light, and what you have whispered in private rooms shall be proclaimed on the housetops.*[17]

## So how do you avoid trouble?

We adhere to the view that the medium and the technology are not the problem, but the heart of the person using them. In this case, the supposed privacy offers a cloak—a

---

[17] Luke 12:2-3 (ESV)

false promise, but that's the pretense—to allow you to indulge your curiosity or lust without immediate consequence. So if the privacy is the problem, away with it.

In short, we share passwords and accounts in our family. We used to have a single email account until Hal became president of our state homeschool association, and the tidal wave of traffic from the non-profit world forced us to start dividing email streams for better handling. Now we simply share *all* our logins and passwords with each other. We go into each other's accounts often enough that no one sees it in the least as snooping (in fact, it's a great convenience to be able to call from the car and say, "Honey, could you email a reply to that message for me?") That goes for our children, too. Anyone who doesn't immediately send their parents the login and password for any online account they have, loses access to the Internet. It's just smart.

The supposed secrecy is too often used by Satan to tempt us to sin, whether looking at inappropriate images or engaging in inappropriate communication. We know of Christian marriages destroyed by "friendships" online that led from confiding secrets to a full-blown affair. Don't get lured in by this. Transparency is the friend of your soul and your marriage!

Likewise, when someone of the opposite sex friends one of us on social media, we send a friend suggestion to our mate after we confirm the friendship. We're just not interested in folks who are threatened by our relationship—we're one, and we tell our friends, "Don't tell me anything you don't want my mate to know—we don't have secrets."

Godly friendships can be a great spur to holiness in the Christian life, *as iron sharpens iron.*[18] The fellowship of believers

---

[18] Proverbs 27:17 (ESV)

is sweet. But friendships need to be made and maintained with wisdom.

## Careless talk

Jesus warned His hearers,

> *"For out of the abundance of the heart the mouth speaks. The good man out of the good treasure of his heart brings forth good things, and an evil man out of the evil treasure brings forth evil things. But I say to you that every for idle word men may speak, they will give account of it in the day of judgment."*[19]

This is something we all have to watch. It is totally socially acceptable, even among Christians to whine about the state of marriage in general and your mate in particular. We were searching online for a quote about marriage, something inspirational, and it was like wading through a cesspool. There were 99 offensive, smart-mouth, hurtful quotes for every one that was sort of okay. One of the problems with careless talk is a condition psychologists call cognitive dissonance. The idea is that if you say something often enough, you start to believe it; your brain doesn't cope well with lies or trying to believe two different things at once. It's said that the disharmony in your thoughts will eventually make you reject one thought for the other. So, if you complain often enough about men or your husband, it becomes a sort of belief or expectation: "Men are pigs." It's time to be careful, *"For as he thinks in his heart, so is he."* [20]

---

[19] Matthew 12: 34-36
[20] Proverbs 23:7a

On the other hand, this can work in your *favor*—if you say the right thing and keep a kindly, civil tongue in your head, your head will eventually follow along. So careless talk should become careful talk.

## How to be in love again

Notice we didn't say *fall* in love again. People talk about love like it was catching the flu, or an accident like tripping over a curb, but that isn't the Biblical view at all!

The English language is not very precise for describing love. In the Greek the New Testament was written in, there are several words for love: *eros* for romantic love, *phileos* for brotherly love, *agape* for sacrificial, godly love, and more. In English, we use the same word for enjoying a cheeseburger or taking a bullet for someone. It's all "love." In the Scripture, love is an action, not a state of being.

What is love? Love is regarding someone else's needs and desires more highly than your own. It's something you can do, something you can practice.

The love of husband and wife should be *all* loves—unconditional, sacrificial *agape*, the love of family and brotherhood of *phileos*, the passionate physical love of *eros*. *All* of them. But in Scripture, they are all *actions*—things you do. Love is not an illness that comes upon you or a truck that strikes you in the street.

## Choose to love

If love is something you can do, it is something you can choose to do. You can choose to regard someone else more highly than yourself. Does that seem like a joyless life of constant sacrifice? You need to remind yourself of the lovable, or likeable things about your mate. You need to regard them more highly. Make a list—what do you "love" about your mate?

If that seems too hard, if your heart has become too cold toward them, try to remember, why did you marry them? It can't be all that hard to find something likeable there. After all, you didn't marry Adolf Hitler or Genghis Khan—and even those men had someone who loved them.

Think about those qualities you admire (or at least remember) about your mate. Look for examples of them. Write down some examples.

## Choose to express love

Look for an opportunity to express admiration or appreciation or gratefulness for one of those traits to your mate. Look for a concrete example, because for some of you that will lend "verisimilitude to an otherwise bald and unconvincing narrative." [21]

Wives should focus on things you respect and admire in your husband. Think about the particularly manly virtues—things like courage, persistence, ambition, integrity, strength, and self-sacrifice. Surely you can find something in their character to praise. If you have trouble with the person he seems to have become, then praise the man he was and could be again.

---

[21] From Gilbert & Sullivan's *Mikado*, 1885. We are devoted Savoyards.

Husbands should particularly focus on things you find lovely, attractive, and winsome about your mate, but *not* at this point overtly sexual. That can seem a little too self-serving if you haven't been doing this before. "That looks great on you" or "Your hair is gorgeous" is fine. "I want to get you in bed," is not. Women do not like to feel used—like you are only after them for your own pleasure, though they do want to feel alluring.

## Expect disbelief

If walls have been built up in your marriage, expect things to get worse before they get better. Often when you start showing love and appreciation, the other person reacts with skepticism or even hostility. You need to remember that defensiveness and disbelief are a defense against getting hurt again. Accept this as the due consequences of your previous neglect and *earn* the right to be believed. It will take a while.

## Practice love

The investment pays off. Through the course of your life, you will spend more time with your mate than any other human being on earth. If you are each putting the other one ahead of themselves, you will both be tendly cared for and loved. That's irresistible. It makes for a marriage that is a haven from the rest of the world—a place of happiness and joy.

From little ways to big ways, put your mate ahead of yourself. Show your love. Act in a loving way. Ask yourself, "How can I please my husband or wife?" Trust the other to look after your needs—it is the best way of all!

*And then God blessed them, and God said to them,*
*"Be fruitful and multiply;*
**fill the earth and subdue it..."**

— Genesis 1:28a

# ~ 6 ~

# The Physical Aspect

*They did, and night is come; and yet we see*
*Formalities retarding thee.*
*What mean these ladies, which—as though*
*They were to take a clock in pieces—go*
*So nicely about the bride?*
*A bride, before a "Good-night" could be said,*
*Should vanish from her clothes into her bed,*
*As souls from bodies steal, and are not spied.*
*But now she's laid ; what though she be?*
*Yet there are more delays, for where is he?*
*He comes and passeth through sphere after sphere;*
*First her sheets, then her arms, then anywhere.*
*Let not this day, then, but this night be thine;*
*Thy day was but the eve to this, O Valentine.*

— John Donne[1]

A few weeks before we were married, we attended a friend's wedding. At the time we were very interested in how they were handling some of the details, but all we remember now is the new groom standing with a few friends outside the reception hall, rhapsodizing over God's gift of marriage. "Ah, the blessings of marriage," he exulted, "both the temporal *as well as* the spiritual!"

---

[1] Donne, John. "An Epithalamion, or Marriage Song on the Lady Elizabeth and Count Palatine Being Married on St. Valentine's Day." Poem. 1613, VI.

Although we still chuckle when we think of his proclamation—with all of twenty minutes' experience behind it—he was right. There are many earthly and spiritual blessings to marriage. We've certainly found it to be so.

## What the Bible Says About Sexuality And Marriage

As a young ministerial student, what our friend did not have in personal experience, he knew from the Word of God and the wise men of church history. The theologians and pastors of the Westminster Assembly, for example, writing the confession adopted by Presbyterian and Reformed churches all over the world, had a remarkable gift for the succinct statement. In chapter 24, they explained marriage in 33 words:

> Marriage was ordained for the mutual help of husband and wife, for the increase of mankind with a legitimate issue, and of the Church with an holy seed; and for preventing of uncleanness.[2]

It's an elegant statement from a theological standpoint. It doesn't stir the soul of most people, but an awful lot of it is about sex.

Now that we have your attention, look back at that statement. They found three features of marriage as God established it—help (for both of you), legitimate children, and legitimate sexual relations. And we would argue that the *third* point is part of the *first*. Remember, God created Eve for Adam, making the observation, "It is *not good that man should be alone.*" [3] It's a help to our moral walk to have a spouse.

---

[2] *Westminster Confession of Faith*, 24:2. The *Second London Baptist Confession* of 1689, adopted by many Baptists in Great Britain and the United States, has almost identical language in its chapter 25.

[3] Genesis 2:18

So all three points have a sexual component and they are all three Biblical, too.

**Marriage is for mutual help:** *And the LORD God said, 'It is not good that man should be alone; I will make him a helper comparable to him.'... Then the rib which the LORD God had taken from man He made into a woman, and He brought her to the man.*[4]

**God gave us to each other to provide legitimate issue:** *Did he not make them one, with a portion of the Spirit in their union? And what was the one God seeking? Godly offspring.*[5]

**Marriage helps prevent sin:** *Nevertheless, because of sexual immorality, let each man have his own wife, and let each woman have her own husband.*[6]

So the Puritans found these three purposes for marriage, and two of them have to do with sexuality—and really, all three.

Christians are often derided as "hung up" about sex. There are good reasons, though not reasons obvious to most of the world. The Bible has a great deal to say about sexuality, and not just "Thou shalt not" statements, or even, "Do this here [*if you must*], but don't do anything else anywhere else ..."

First, our sexuality is a core feature of our individual being. God created man and woman as sexually differentiated creatures from the very beginning, before there was sin and imperfection in the world:

---

[4] Genesis 2:18, 22
[5] Malachi 2:15 (ESV)
[6] 1 Corinthians 7:2

> *So God created man in His own image; in the image of God He created him; male and female He created them. Then God blessed them, and God said to them, "Be fruitful and multiply; fill the earth and subdue it... "... Then God saw everything that He had made, and indeed it was very good...*[7]

By the way, that's the first commandment recorded in scripture—to be fruitful and multiply, the man and woman would have to come together. So if our most fundamental nature is shaped by sexuality and the sexual union, it makes sense we would make much of it.

Other passages speak of the delights of marital love:

> *...rejoice with the wife of your youth. As a loving deer and a graceful doe, Let her breasts satisfy you at all times; And always be enraptured with her love.*[8]

> *He who finds a wife finds a good thing, And obtains favor from the LORD.*[9]

> *Live joyfully with the wife whom you love all the days of your vain life...*[10]

---

[7] Genesis 1:27-28, 31

[8] Proverbs 5:18-19. It's interesting to note that this is one of the few passages in Scripture which alludes to keeping pets, that is, animals for companionship and beauty rather than sheer utility. See descriptions of King Solomon's commerce in apes and monkeys [or peacocks, in the ESV] (1 Kings 10:22, 2 Chronicles 9:21), and the poor man's pet lamb in the prophet Nathan's parable (2 Samuel 12:3).

[9] Proverbs 18:22

[10] Ecclesiastes 9:9. Granted, the writer of Ecclesiastes (presumably Solomon) was working from an existential crisis, hence the cry of "vanity", but even then, you see how God often blesses unbelievers as well as His children with this earthly joy.

*So husbands ought to love their own wives as their own bodies; he who loves his wife loves himself.... "For this reason a man shall leave his father and mother and be joined to his wife, and the two shall become one flesh."... let each of you in particular so love his own wife as himself...*[11]

And that's not even touching the Song of Solomon, a section of Scripture so poetic and descriptive of the raptures of a bride and groom that rabbis used to counsel young men not to read it until they were thirty years old.

No, the Bible is not prudish or hung up about sex; it is very much in favor of it—within the context of marriage. And just to balance the positive side of the question, there's another reason to take this seriously—because sexual immorality is a different class of sin:

*Flee sexual immorality. Every sin that a man does is outside the body, but he who commits sexual immorality sins against his own body.*[12]

The apostle Paul wrote this to the church at Corinth, a city so notorious for its sexual abandon that the Greek language had a word for fornication, *korinthiázomai*, literally "to act Corinthian." [13] Converts coming into the church from the port-city culture around them had a lot to learn. *[B]ecause of*

---

[11] Ephesians 5:28,31,33

[12] 1 Corinthians 6:18

[13] "Κορινθι-άζομαι, A. practise fornication, because Corinth was famous for its courtesans, Aristophanes, *Fragment 354:*—Act. in Hsch." (Henry George Liddell. Robert Scott. *A Greek-English Lexicon.* revised and augmented throughout by. Sir Henry Stuart Jones. with the assistance of. Roderick McKenzie. Oxford. Clarendon Press. 1940. ‹http://www.perseus.tufts.edu/hopper/text?doc=Perseus%3Atext%3A1999.04.0057%3Aentry%3D*korinqia%2Fzomai›, accessed 8/28/12.)

*sexual immorality,* Paul wrote a few verses later, *let each man have his own wife, and let each woman have her own husband.*"[14] Surrounded by the raging carnality of Corinthian society, where prostitution was a religious act and business affairs and social events were held in the dining rooms of brothels (masquerading as temples), Paul pointed the believer to the God-ordained protection—the arms of his or her spouse.

## Much grief in the world because of misuse of this gift

There is no debating that our culture's changing views of sexuality have brought about disturbing trends in marriage. Here in the U.S., there are fewer and later marriages than we once saw. Among working class American adults, the marriage rate has fallen from 84% in 1960 to less than 50% today.[15] Cohabitation rates, on the other hand, have soared. Some 60% of American women ages 25-40 have lived with a boyfriend before (or instead of) marriage.[16] Children are bearing the burden, too. Since 1970 the percentage of children born out of wedlock has gone from just over 10% to more than 40%, in 2008.[17] Research has shown that children born

---

[14] 1 Corinthians 7:2

[15] Murray, Charles. "The New American Divide." *Wall Street Journal* [New York] 21 Jan 2012, Saturday n. pag. Web. 29 Aug. 2012. ‹http://online.wsj.com/article/SB10001424052970204301404577170733817181646.html›.

[16] Kennedy, Sheela, and Larry Bumpass. "Cohabitation and children's living arrangements: New estimates from the United States." *Demographic Research*. 19. (2008): 1663-1692. Web. 29 Aug. 2012. ‹http://www.demographic-research.org/volumes/vol19/47/19-47.pdf›.

[17] Table 7, "Nonmarital childbearing, by detailed race and Hispanic origin of mother, and maternal age: United States, selected years 1970-2008", p. 83. National Center for Health Statistics. *Health, United States, 2011: With Special Feature on Socioeconomic Status and Health.* Hyattsville, MD. 2012. Web. 29 Aug. 2012. ‹http://www.cdc.gov/nchs/data/hus/hus11.pdf#007›.

out of wedlock fare much worse, on nearly every measure, than children born into two-parent families.[18]

Several factors have played into this change. Economically, the expansion of federal and state social welfare programs have made it *appear* easier for single mothers to get along without a husband and father in the picture. The reality is quite different, as single parents struggle to provide economic security for their children.[19] But where concern for their support may have encouraged young women to think hard before agreeing to a young man's ring-less proposition, the safety net has taken some of the fear that may have guided that decision.

Our generation was the first raised with a completely secular education. Melanie's mother was led to Christ by a public school Bible teacher, but by the time we were in school it was daring to pray or refer to the Bible in any way. Cultural Christianity cannot substitute for actual faith and a living church, but it can inform the society of standards for right and wrong and set the tone for the community. This erosion of a cultural consensus that sex outside of marriage was simply immoral, period, coincides with other changes which have landed us right where we are as a society.

Even earlier, the Protestant church's acceptance of contraception "for sufficiently grave reasons" in the early 1930's opened the door for greater access to birth control. By lowering the risks of unintended pregnancy, another restraint to unbridled sexual adventurism was removed. The legalization

---

[18] . "Births to Unmarried Women." *Child Trends Databank*. Child Trends, Mar 2012. Web. 29 Aug 2012. ‹www.childtrendsdatabank.org/?q=node/196›.

[19] Waldfogel, Jane, Terry-Ann Craigie, and Jeanne Brooks-Gunn. "Fragile Families and Child Wellbeing." *Future Child*. 20.2 (2010): 87-112. Web. 29 Aug. 2012. ‹http://www.ncbi.nlm.nih.gov/pmc/articles/PMC3074431/pdf/nihms-273444.pdf›.

of abortion in *Roe v. Wade* made this even worse, offering a "backstop" position if contraception failed to prevent "accidents." Thankfully, many women with an unplanned pregnancy find they don't have the heart to carry through with an abortion, saving the life of the child but also contributing to the increasing birth rate outside of wedlock.

It's sad. This culture of promiscuity, abandonment, death, and despair are *not* the pattern God has given us for sexuality.

As the culture has continued down this path, the church has had its share of stumbling as well. Perhaps in reaction to licentiousness in the culture at large—an ongoing problem, whether considering 1st century Rome or 21st century America—sometimes the church has elevated celibacy as an ideal or higher calling. Jesus made it plain that celibacy was a particular gift, not a higher state. When He taught about divorce, His disciples protested, *"If such is the case of the man with his wife, it is better not to marry."* Jesus replied, *"All cannot accept this saying, but only those to whom it has been given."* [20]

Instead, we read that *Marriage is honorable among all, and the bed undefiled.* [21]

Some in the church have erred by emphasizing procreation as the major purpose for sexuality, ignoring extended passages in places like the Song of Solomon which clearly celebrate the righteous enjoyment of pleasure in one another. The Proverbs call marital love *ravishing, enrapturing, captivating, intoxicating,* or *exhilarating.* [22]

---

[20] Matthew 19:10-11
[21] Hebrews 13:4
[22] Proverbs 5:19, as rendered in KJV, NKJV, NIV, ESV, and NASB, respectively.

But in these liberated and sexually saturated days, it is more often that the church has fallen into the world's way of thinking about sexuality. Instead of acknowledging that God created the marital union for both pleasure and pregnancy, we follow the world's lead and try to keep the sexual act and the conception of children as separate as possible.

We may talk about the blessing of children occasionally, seeing as it's in the Psalms and all, but like the world, we tend to think more about fertility as a risky side effect of our intimate fun.

The world's view of sexuality, where it's not actively evil, is unbalanced at its core. Our family enjoys the flavors of international foods, and occasionally we treat ourselves with a stop at an Indian restaurant. Most we visit serve buffet style, and we have a positive relish for curries, *biryanis*, and *dahls*. Hal is the typical meat-and-potatoes guy, but always remarks, "If I ever had to go totally vegetarian, I could do this."

But life is not lived in constant feasting, a blazing barrage of cream, peppers, coriander and *garam masala*—even in India. Neither is our sexuality intended to be a non-stop buffet of exotica, with our personal pleasure of the moment being the predominating focus. Down that path lie hedonism, egocentrism, and a desire for conquest and domination—the triumph of one's will over another's—rather than a expression of love, oneness, and commitment. Why would the world use sexual epithets as insults and curses, when the Christian is told to consider the marital union as a picture of Christ and the church?

## We Might Not See The Worldliness Creeping In

B eing bombarded by the world's view from the time we can focus our eyes, we need to be very alert to its influence on our thinking. Striving to overcome too much reluctance to discuss these matters, perhaps, the church may be giving a backhanded approval to some of the worldly expectations. We know to steer clear of outright adultery, maybe, but don't see some of the underlying issues we've simply absorbed and adopted from the culture around us.

Take, for example, our expectations of the sexual act. When we were newlyweds, we read several books by well-respected Christian authors, attempting to counsel people like us and steer us clear of secular sexologists. Certainly, we learned some interesting and occasionally helpful things about physiology and psychology of both of us. It's good to get that information from a source which respects God's purpose and design in creating us.

But all of these books had advice which we later found to be problematic. Most of them seemed to spend a lot of time on what you might call performance issues—not just sexual dysfunctions, though those are there—but more of the scorekeeping variety. And we use the word "score" advisedly. They left us wondering, "Are we doing this right? Are we reaching the proper levels of enjoyment? How does our sexual achievement match up to our goals?"

It can make the marital relationship into a sporting event, and make us into athletes in training, or spectators of our own love affair.

It led us to realize one of the important things we wish we'd understood at first.

## Your Love Life Only Has To Please Three People

That spectator experience made us sit back and think. If we are putting ourselves against a standard, whose? If husband and wife are happy and God is pleased, then that settles it, doesn't it?

It doesn't matter what the national average is, or the prevailing wisdom, or the neighborhood standard, or the advice of the author. God's word is our only external standard, and it's mighty broad. Beyond that, who cares? We aren't selling tickets. Hopefully we've matured out of the Monday-afternoon-in-the-locker-room kind of conversation some folks had in high school, sharing gossip and braggadocio about their weekend romances. If no one but us and the all-seeing God have the slightest awareness of our intimacies, then what do we care what the world's opinion might be?

The other side of that, of course, is that other people's sex lives are none of *our* business either. When the Jesus admonishes, *"whoever looks at a woman to lust for her has already committed adultery with her in his heart,"* [23] and the Proverbs say, of *the wife of your youth,* to *let her breasts satisfy you at all times,*[24] then the question of pornography has already been addressed. Yet there are some additional things which need to be said.

Tim Challies observes that since the rise of the Internet, "it is actually far more difficult to avoid pornography than it is to find it."

> *[When] I meet a young man, even a young husband,*
> *I pretty much assume he either is or was into por-*

---

[23] Matthew 5:28
[24] Proverbs 5:18-19

*nography. I honestly don't think that's unrealistic, unfair, or cynical. It's the accessibility problem... Porn is so prevalent that it's nearly certain every young man will find it; and once it has been tasted, it is difficult not to indulge.[25]*

It has become so pervasive that it is influencing popular culture. Images and behavior which were considered edgy and risqué a few decades ago are becoming commonplace, lifted into view by the tide of sewage rising beneath them.

God gave us six sons first, then our daughters. We have finally discovered for ourselves what we heard many Christian parents complain about—that it is difficult to find clothing for a six- or seven-year-old girl which doesn't look like the sort of outfits favored by the campus flirts of our college days. Who thought it would be appropriate to print a double-entendre across the seat of a young girl's sweat suit? Why should my third grader dress like a sorority pledge ten years older? It's a symptom of a disturbing taste which is being cultivated in secret but is creeping more boldly into the daylight.

Of course, it's not just sexualizing little girls. The industry of making women into objects is polluting our whole understanding of beauty. Recently one of the top models approached a news outlet to ask if they would publish her unretouched photo from a recent studio session, next to the finished, polished-up image. It was startling to see that someone said to be one of the world's most beautiful women didn't look anything close to the perfected image we saw of her in the media.

---

[25] Challies, Tim. *Sexual Detox: A Guide for Guys Who Are Sick of Porn.* Adelphi, MD: Cruciform Press, 2010. 12, 25. eBook.

The images of women in advertising has gone beyond an earlier year's airbrush pimple-removal to wholesale re-engineering of the female form. Melanie has made a bit of a study of it, and it's shocking how the digitally-altered images in advertisements and catalogs present a figure no woman could stand—literally: one recent ad campaign had trimmed a model's hips so smooth there was no room for a pelvis. Where do her legs connect? Bet that's an interesting x-ray.

At least no one dies from digital manipulation; the promotion of extremely thin fashion models has resulted in at least one death and is blamed for the continued rise of anorexia in young women.

The sad result of this imagery is a cultural preference for a female figure which is difficult, dangerous, or impossible to attain, an unrealistic expectation in the eyes of men, and a self-doubt in the hearts of women. Alarmingly, that preference for women who appear to be pre-pubescent also may lead our culture down even more perverted paths which endanger children.

Likewise, the behavior shown in pornography (and in a lesser form, in popular media generally) influences how we see one another and what we expect from our mates. Even if we virtuously resolve to keep our thoughts on our wife or husband and not on the images we've seen or the books we've read, we misjudge what real life and real people are like. A generation ago, researchers found that avid soap opera fans tended to overestimate the number of doctors, lawyers, extramarital affairs, and illegitimate children in society.[26]

[26] Greenberg, Bradley S., Kimberly Neuendorf, Nancy Buerkel-Rothfuss, and Laura Henderson. "The Soaps: What's On and Who Cares?" *Journal of Broadcasting*. 26.2 (1982): 519-535 . Print. <http://academic.csuohio.edu/kneuendorf/vitae/GreenbergNeuendorfBuerkel-Rothfussetal82.pdf>. Given

In the same way, if our attitudes and expectations of the marriage bed are informed by popular culture or worse, we will bring unrealistic (and unreachable) standards to our mates.

## We're So Used To Sin, We Don't Need To Rehearse It Any More

Melanie recently read a question online from a Christian wife, a mother, who was concerned that her husband wanted her to be restrained for physical relations. She ought to be concerned! That sort of "play" is pretending at rape. Where in the Bible do you find sexual assault as a part of marriage? Why should a wife, in a different scenario, be expected to give in to ideas which are degrading and offensive, taking the role of harlot, or else pushing back against her husband's advances? Why should a husband find pleasure in pretending to violate his own bride?

Yet, this kind of behavior may become more common. The prevalence of violent and perverted pornography seems to be changing people's standards. Shockingly, nearly a quarter of male college students admitted to being so sexually aggressive that they'd caused "their date to cry, scream or plead." [27]

Should we play at that? No! Rather, the Word warns us that sin is no laughing matter and nothing to play around with. *Fools mock at sin*, warns the proverb, and *to do evil* is *like sport to a fool*. [28] From the Old Testament and from the lips of Jesus we learn that while man only judges by what he can see, God looks on the heart, and a heart which is inclined

---

the skyrocketing number of unmarried parents, you might wonder if it's still possible to overestimate the rate of illegitimacy.

[27] Javed, Noor. "Insight." *TheStar.com*. Toronto Star Newspapers, Ltd., 22 Apr. 2013. Web. 08 May 2013.

[28] Proverbs 14:9, 10:23

toward a gross, outward sin has already crossed the line in the area seen by God alone:

> For the LORD does not see as man sees; for man looks at the outward appearance, but the LORD looks at the heart.

> "You have heard that it was said to those of old, 'You shall not murder...' But I say to you that whoever is angry with his brother without a cause shall be in danger of the judgment. And whoever says to his brother, 'Raca!' ["You good-for-nothing!" (NASB)] shall be in danger of the council. But whoever says, 'You fool!' shall be in danger of hell fire ...

> "You have heard that it was said to those of old, 'You shall not commit adultery.' But I say to you that whoever looks at a woman to lust for her has already committed adultery with her in his heart." [29]

That doesn't minimize the grosser crimes at all, but tells us God takes our inner thoughts and fantasies much more seriously that we probably do. And if God sees our casual ogling across the neighbor's pool fence as adultery in our spirit, then we have to consider that playing at rape is much the same thing—a heart which delights in assault and domination.

We're not big fans of Halloween—for the same reasons, come to think of it; why would we dress the children God gave us as if they were servants of the Prince of Hell?—but beyond the supernatural aspect, we are seeing a serious downward trend in the costume aisles. The costumes for women, and even young girls, tend to be highly sexualized

---

[29] Matthew 5:28

—"naughty" nurses, suggestive schoolgirl uniforms, servant's costumes, and worse. What are they suggesting? Pedophilia, perversions of different sorts, wealthy men taking advantage of their household staff. It's simple—they are playing at sin, even if they're "safely married."

Besides, we're so good at falling into the real thing, why would we go role-playing "notorious" sinner? Even if Jesus hadn't warned us, it seems like we get enough practice on our own without acting out a make-believe scandal.

Why are we tempted to do these things? Probably because sinful acts carry the risk of being caught, and our tempters whisper the ancient refrain, *Stolen water is sweet, and bread eaten in secret is pleasant.*[30] Beyond that, though, is the tempter's lie that familiar intimacies with the same person, year after year, will grow boring and mundane. It's patently false, yet every worldly magazine is screaming from their covers, the latest list of secrets which will breathe new thrills into your sad, sad, sex life.

Don't buy it.

## The Problem of Just Looking

There was a country song several years ago where the singer assures his jealous wife that although he had wandering eyes, he was "just looking"; his heart was firmly at home. The problem is, that's not Biblical, and it works even less as an excuse for pornography.

The righteous (if troubled) Job says at one point, "*I have made a covenant with my eyes; Why then should I look upon a*

---

[30] Proverbs 9:17

*young woman?"*[31] In view of his marriage, he isn't going out to gaze on virgins, as the English Standard Version renders it—even though polygamy was still permitted in the culture.

Job understood, as Jesus made explicit at the Sermon on the Mount, that enjoying the thrill of desire for an attractive young body other than his wife's was a violation of his marriage vows. Neither Job nor Jesus are confining their remarks to the lecherous beach-goer, ogling the co-eds with binoculars, nor to the foolish youth described in Proverbs 7, following the seductive woman to her bed. Just checking out an unsuspecting young woman going about her normal business could be Job's own pathway to sin.

Lust is a corrosive, consuming sin, and it starts small. It starts young, too. A few years ago, we read a study from the University of New Hampshire, where incoming freshmen (both men and women) were asked about their experience of Internet pornography. While both had been exposed, fully 93% of the 18-year-old men admitted to seeing porn online, and 69% had actively sought it out and watched it. Nearly a third, 29%, said they were first exposed when they were 13 or younger.[32]

And that's in the U.S., which much of the world considers hopelessly prudish about sex. It's as bad or worse in other places.

> *A British survey published by* Psychologies *magazine in 2010 found that 81 per cent of 14-to-16-year-olds (regardless of gender) had looked at porn*

[31] Job 31:1

[32] Chiara, Sabina, Janis Wolak, and David Finkelhor. "The Nature and Dynamics of Internet Pornography Exposure for Youth." *CyberPsychology & Behavior.* 11.6 (2008): n. page. Web. 2 Sep. 2012 <http://www.unh.edu/ccrc/pdf/CV169.pdf>.

*online at home while 63 per cent called it up on their phones; a third of them had seen sexual images online when they were 10 or younger. A 2006 study involving rural Alberta youth from 17 schools found that 88 per cent of Grade 8 boys [14-year-olds] had viewed porn online...*[33]

Men need to discipline themselves to look away from temptation, no matter where they find it. That may mean skipping the commercials on the Super Bowl, studying the candy bar display in the checkout line to avoid the tabloid rack, or even keeping a very formal relationship with a co-worker at the office. It may mean mowing the backyard only when the neighbor isn't enjoying her pool—or calling it a day on the yardwork if she comes out. God made men very responsive to visual stimulation, and men have to take seriously their commitment to their wives and to their Lord. There is more than one covenant in place, you see.

## The physical danger of pornography

When the product is pornography, there's not even the minimal excuse of "accidentally" seeing a tempting image in a commercial or advertisement. Its sole purpose is to excite sexual desire, or at least, the desire to purchase more and more expensive images. Its goal is your lust. Pornographers have no concern about your spiritual well-being; if they successfully lure you into their trap, leading you into repeated acts of spiritual adultery, that's your problem.

---

[33] Bielski, Zosia. "In the age of Internet porn, teaching boys to be good men." *Globe and Mail* [Toronto, Ontario] 21 Apr 2012, Saturday n. pag. Web. 2 Sep. 2012. <http://www.theglobeandmail.com/life/parenting/teens/sexuality/in-the-age-of-internet-porn-teaching-boys-to-be-good-men/article2409690/>.

But if the spiritual danger weren't enough, research is revealing a physical danger as well. The sight of a stimulating image, whether the wife of your youth or a porn queen online, causes the body to produce dopamine, the hormone which mediates sexual arousal in the brain. Because Internet pornography can be displayed and changed at a rapid rate, the user can quickly overstimulate himself; like pupils contracting in bright light, the brain's dopamine receptors desensitize to protect themselves against the unnatural onslaught of hormones. This means the pornography user must seek higher and higher levels of stimulation to experience the same level of arousal. As the sin increases, so does the desensitization.

Researchers are now reporting frequent cases of sexual dysfunction and impotence among young men in their twenties. Some of these are young husbands who find they can't respond to their wives, as much as they wish to. Eventually even the extremes of pornography are unable to break through their calloused response.[34] Doctors say that complete abstinence for as long as two to six months may restore sensitivity—a difficult prescription for a man habituated to constant, over-the-top sexual titillation.

The apostle Paul warned the church in Corinth,

> *Flee sexual immorality. Every sin that a man does is outside the body, but he who commits sexual immorality sins against his own body.*[35]

How sad to discover, twenty-one centuries later, yet another way immorality leads to physical harm.[36]

---

34 Robinson, Marnia. "Porn-Induced Sexual Dysfunction Is a Growing Problem." *Psychology Today*. Psychology Today, 11 July 2011. Web. 25 Aug. 2012.

35 1 Corinthians 6:18

36 The other danger is the "cranial EGDOL" problem. Hal is convinced that if he indulged a temptation of this sort, he could expect a permanent

And we shouldn't forget ever, that participation in this industry fosters exploitation and abuse of real women and real girls, and cheapens the culture's view of womanhood. This is not a victimless sin, it hurts everyone it touches. Don't even start down that path, not the first step. And if you're already down that road, get help and get out.

## Women's Temptations

Women have their own temptations, too. Sadly, a growing number of women are becoming addicted to Internet pornography, with the same kinds of effects the men experience. Studies referenced earlier record that girls are not immune to the onslaught of pornography—they just seem to fall less frequently than the boys.

More commonly, though, just as men are drawn to images, women are drawn to emotions. Long before there were "beefcake" magazines for women to lust over, there were romance novels and romantic movies.

Every generation seems to have its worst-ever example of "mommy porn," as the current bestseller has been called. One of Hal's teachers in high school, a very proper and very conservative woman with a sharp eye for cultural trends, told of overhearing a conversation at the circulation desk of the library. A prim, elderly woman was sheepishly returning a scandalous novel.

"Why, Miss ————, I wouldn't have expected *you* to be reading this," said the librarian.

---

imprint of the trademark from Melanie's iron skillet, as made by the Lodge Manufacturing Company of South Pittsburg, Tennessee.

Blushing bright scarlet, the embarrassed spinster stuttered, "But... it's so beautifully *written*."

Once upon a time, men who knew better claimed they only read *Playboy* for the articles, too.

The current blight on the literary world is an explicit story of a sado-masochistic relationship—one book even has the effrontery to display a pair of handcuffs for the cover art. Its popularity suggests the same kind of escalation we were talking about among men watching online porn is very likely happening among women. It's just a different stimulation.

We hear about men encouraging their wives to read trashy novels like this in the hopes that it will increase their desire. Really, it's likely to do the opposite in the long run. Just like no real woman can compete with the altered images of the Internet, neither can any real man be as rich, handsome, powerful, and aristocratic as the protagonist of a novel.

## Repentence

When the apostle Paul speaks to the oversexed culture in Corinth, he lays out a depressing list of lifestyles leading to condemnation:

> *Do you not know that the unrighteous will not inherit the kingdom of God? Do not be deceived. Neither fornicators, nor idolaters, nor adulterers, nor homosexuals, nor sodomites, nor thieves, nor covetous, nor drunkards, nor revilers, nor extortioners will inherit the kingdom of God.*

It's no coincidence that four of the first five are sexual in nature. *And such were some of you*, he continues (ouch),

*But you were washed, but you were sanctified, but
you were justified in the name of the Lord Jesus
and by the Spirit of our God.*[37]

As damaging as sexual immorality can be to body, spirit,
and relationships all around, it is not final, nor irredeemable.
There is a way out, through the forgiveness and restoration
which Jesus can give. But it takes repentance to lay hold of
that.

How can you do that? First, you have to confess your sin
and commit to change. Repentance is about a radical change
of direction, and part of repentance is doing something to
stop. This is the time to get real accountability.[38] Make sure
that someone you respect will be notified if you seek out
sin on the net.

Commit yourself to fighting temptation, too. In our book,
*Raising Real Men*, we talk about how we teach our children
"The Five Fingered Fist to Fight Temptation" and it works just
as well for adults as it does children. When confronted with
temptation, we tell them, take five steps:

**1. Pray:** Seek the Lord's help to overcome the temptation.

*No temptation has overtaken you except such as
is common to man; but God is faithful, who will
not allow you to be tempted beyond what you are
able, but with the temptation will also make the
way of escape, that you may be able to bear it.*[39]

---

[37] 1 Corinthians 6:9-11

[38] We recommend Covenant Eyes. ‹www.CovenantEyes.com› Use the
code **raisingrealmen** to try it free for a month.

[39] 1 Corinthians 10:13

**2. Sing praises to God:** Music engages the heart even when we are feeling very cold and blue, spiritually, and it can draw us closer to God as we remember His grace, love, holiness and power.

> *And whenever the harmful spirit from God was upon Saul, David took the lyre and played it with his hand. So Saul was refreshed and was well, and the harmful spirit departed from him.*[40]

**3. Read the Bible.**

> *Your word I have hidden in my heart, That I might not sin against You.*[41]

**4. Leave the Situation.** At the computer? Close it and get moving. In the shower? Dry off and get out. Alone? Get in a room with other people.

> *Flee also youthful lusts; but pursue righteousness, faith, love, peace with those who call on the Lord out of a pure heart.*[42]

**5. Go to Your Authority.** For adults, this means our mates (remember, God has given us authority over our mate's body) and our pastors. Go to someone who will counsel with you, pray for you, and give you practical advice.

> *Though one may be overpowered by another, two can withstand him. And a threefold cord is not quickly broken.*[43]

---

40 1 Samuel 16:23 (ESV)
41 Psalm 119:11
42 2 Timothy 2:22
43 Ecclesiastes 4:12

These five ways to fight are like a fist that knocks away temptation!

The only way to deal with sexual sin is no excuses, no tolerance, a complete fast. It's an addiction, physical and spiritual, and you need to BREAK it. You don't give an alcoholic a drink, you help him fight the craving.

## But are we doing this right?

There are obvious traps that many fall into, and we've tried to talk about the real troubles and some help to avoid them or escape them. Thankfully, the physical relationship is not all a listen of *watch-out* and *don't-dare* and *avoid-at-all-cost* instructions. After all, it's supposed to be a fountain of joy to a husband and wife.[44]

Hopefully, you're not reading this chapter in the hopes of finding a Christian sex manual. If you started at the beginning, you can guess we're not going to offer you one. And really, God created you for one another, in part for this very thing—glorifying God in your bodies, by enjoying one another in obedience to His command, and quite probably bringing a new generation of His servants into the world.

It's not that hard to figure out, and really, the finer points are something that the two of you need to figure out yourselves. Recognize that a lot of the advice you'll see, whether in person or more likely in print somewhere, has come from people with too much baggage and jaded tastes. Especially if you are coming to this as virgins, it's a land of pure delight.

If *you're* the one with baggage and jaded tastes, you may need to rethink a lot of what you believe about sexuality, in

[44] Proverbs 5:18

order to begin to think about it Biblically. You may need to seek forgiveness of God. You may need to abstain from thinking about certain things. You need to remake your mind, but our God is the one who restores the years the locust have eaten.[45]

And remember the Israelites on their way to the Promised Land. Don't volunteer to go back to Egypt. If God has set you on a pathway of fulfillment, both of your own desires and of His will, then don't let the world or people around you put conditions and expectations on you. Don't let them lead you to dissatisfaction and discontent.

## Love Life Changes—And That's Okay

Most of us come to our marriage with great expectations, and the anticipation of the honeymoon is high on the list. It's a milestone time which is not to be minimized. In ancient Israel, a man received a one-year exemption from the draft when he took a wife—in fact, he was exempt during his engagement, too:

> So it shall be, when you are on the verge of a battle…the officers shall speak to the people, saying: … what man is there who is betrothed to a woman and has not married her? Let him go and return to his house, lest he die in battle and another man marry her.[46]

> When a man has taken a new wife, he shall not go out to war or be charged with any business; he shall be free at home one year, and bring happiness to his wife whom he has taken.[47]

---

[45] Joel 2:25
[46] Deuteronomy 20:2,5,7
[47] Deuteronomy 24:5

But honestly, there is usually a lot of uncertainly and anxiety during that time, too. For all its special memories, there will be plenty of times over the years to come that will be more passionate and enjoyable than any hour of your honeymoon could have been. At other times, job separation or illness or some other reason may make your time together rare and unusual.

It's all okay as long as both of you can be patient and content with the situation.

The news media had a little stir last year over a Christian author's challenge to couples in a stale or almost troubled relationship, to commit to making love every single day for a period of several weeks (or even longer). Is that a Biblical goal, or a world-teasing stunt?

It's probably somewhere in between. The Bible doesn't give specifics, but Paul indicated the answer is *regularly*:

> *[Because] of sexual immorality, let each man have his own wife, and let each woman have her own husband. Let the husband render to his wife the affection due her, and likewise also the wife to her husband. The wife does not have authority over her own body, but the husband does. And likewise the husband does not have authority over his own body, but the wife does. Do not deprive one another except with consent for a time, that you may give yourselves to fasting and prayer; and come together again so that Satan does not tempt you because of your lack of self-control.*[48]

---

[48] 1 Corinthians 7:2-5

So a couple should be intimate often enough to head off temptation for either of them. That word, "intimate," has two meanings, and they both apply. On the one side, there should be regular sexual relations, to address the temptations of immorality; but there should also be a strong and frequently renewed emotional intimacy, as we discuss in another chapter. Neither one is the primary domain of one partner; both husbands and wives need both physical and emotional unity, on an ongoing basis.

As Ecclesiastes says, there is *A time to embrace, And a time to refrain from embracing*.[49] While we are freed from the requirements of the Mosaic law, it's instructive that the Levitical code fenced off certain times for abstaining, such as during the normal monthly cycle and several weeks after childbirth.[50] If either spouse had any sort of discharge, that time was treated like the woman's period.[51] It would seem that considering both Paul's instruction and God's law in the nation of Israel, there is plenty of justification for abstaining for health or for special, devotional reasons. That, in itself, says the love-every-day challenge probably steps over a line; even if ritual impurity is no longer a consideration, it's more kind to the wife especially to leave off for a few days when she's indisposed.

Beyond that, though, it's up to you—and it will vary as your day-to-day circumstances vary. As we said, this whole area is between husband, wife, and God. There's no scoreboard in the bedroom.

---

[49] Ecclesiastes 3:5
[50] Leviticus 18:19, 12:2-5
[51] Leviticus 15:1-33

## Passion Has A Place, But Not All of It

The church, as well as the rabbis, has sometimes been a bit cautious about the Song of Solomon. Some commentators scurried away from the romantic language and waxed lyrical about the love of Christ for His bride, the church—which certainly may be an accurate reading. Yet if the Song is primarily or only an allegory of the Savior and His people, even so God used very powerful and evocative language to describe it! Surely He would not have blessed an unholy passion by describing the mystery of Christ and the Church in this way.

But reading the book as literal, it *is* romantic. The narrative of courtship, betrothal, and nuptials is poetic, exotic, and yes, even erotic at times. There can be no question that passion has a big place within the bounds of marriage.

And yet, it's not all passion all the time, like a satellite radio station with only one theme. There are those times of separation and abstinence, as we said. There is also a different sort of married love in Scripture.

Consider the case of Isaac and Rebekah. When famine drove them to the Philistine city of Gerar, Isaac committed the same sin as his father Abraham—he lied about their relationship and claimed Rebekah was his sister, not his wife, in hope that no one would kill him to take his bride.

> *And it came to pass, when he had been there a long time, that Abimelech king of the Philistines looked out at a window, and saw, and, behold, Isaac was sporting with Rebekah his wife. And Abimelech called Isaac, and said, Behold, of a surety she is thy wife: and how saidst thou, She is my sister?* [52]

---

[52] Genesis 26:8-9 (KJV)

They were "sporting"—and what was that?

It was something intimate enough that Abimelech knew they weren't brother and sister, but innocent enough they might chance it in public. The Hebrew word means "laughing"—it was intimate, but playful. Some translations say "caressing."

The world might say that all your time together should be earth-shaking passion, or heart stopping romance. The Bible shows us it can be both of those, or it can be affectionate, or playful, or comfortable, or profound—at different times in different ways. Different cycles of life will affect this too—different parts of the monthly cycle, different parts of the child-bearing cycle, different times of life.

## Other things might affect you

Melanie remembers her friend, Emily,[53] coming to her with a very serious concern.

"I don't think I love Chad any more!" she burst out.

Melanie asked her why in the world she would say that; why in the world she would *think* that.

"I just have no desire at all for Chad! I have never felt this way before, but I don't feel anything. I don't have any thoughts of making love at all!" Emily said.

Melanie suddenly recalled that though they had several children, the new baby was the first one she'd breastfed.

---

[53] Names have been changed to protect the couple's privacy in this sensitive area.

"Oh, Emily!" Melanie exclaimed. "You haven't fallen out of love. It's just your hormones!"

Melanie has been a lactation consultant for many years, and she recognized Emily's symptoms. The hormones associated with nursing sometimes make the mother feel like she couldn't even remember why people *do* that anyway. If Emily would just make herself open to her husband's advances, Melanie suggested, she would almost certainly respond like always, though perhaps a little slower, and enjoy it just as much.

A few days later, Emily stopped by the house.

"Oh thank you, thank you, thank you!" Emily cheered. "I had no idea! I thought it was all over, but now that I understand... well, it was just great! Chad is so happy, too!"

Pregnancy can do the same thing, while some women find their libido actually increases when they're expecting. Sometimes sickness will mean a time of lessened or no relations. We talk about this more in the chapter on sickness and health. A wife's hysterectomy or having her tubes tied, or a husband's vasectomy, can decrease desire, too. It's a process profoundly involved with hormones, and anything which changes the hormonal balance is likely to change your interest in relations—up or down.

Our friend Abigail,[54] for example, had her tubes tied when she and her husband Phil believed their family was complete. For some time afterward, she bounced from doctor to doctor with female problems and a complete lack of desire. Finally she realized that all this started with the sterilization. She

---

[54] Names have been changed to protect the couple's privacy in this sensitive area.

began doing research and asking questions, and finally she approached Phil and suggested she undergo a reversal.

He was shocked, and worried that they might get pregnant again. Abigail wisely stopped talking about it and started praying. About a year later, out of the blue, Phil said to her, "Hey, weren't you going to set it up to have a reversal?" When he also said he was open to more children, Abigail was ecstatic; her own heart had been leaning that direction more and more.

The surgeon who performed the reversal found that the tubal ligation had restricted the blood flow to her ovaries, resulting in her hormonal difficulties. After the reversal, she began to recover, and while the Lord only gave them one more child, that young man was to become a light of their life and a Christian with a worldwide testimony.

## Don't use your affection and attention as bargaining chips.

In college, some of our classmates encountered the Greek play *Lysistrata*. In the ancient narrative, the women of Athens and other Greek cities conspire to withhold their sexual attention from their husbands and lovers until the men agree to settle and end a costly war.

It's not a Biblical response, though, and some couples get themselves into conflict because they try and use sex as a tool to manipulate each other. Paul told the Corinthians that the bodies of the husband and wife each belong to the other, and urged them not to stay long apart, he was aiming for that goal of "preventing uncleanness."[55] When we let ourselves get too busy, too distracted, or too misdirected to spend time

---

[55] 1 Corinthians 7:3-5

together physically, we open the door to temptation. God expects us to be lovers, and to be regular about it.

So how can we rightfully use our affections to manipulate, control, or punish one another? We can't. If the lack of affection wasn't treacherous enough for our spiritual life, we mix in anger and resentment between us!

Instead, let's work towards sacrificing ourselves for the other. In the end, it leads toward happiness for both.

## For your love is better than wine [56]

If the front covers in the magazine racks were an indication, the entire population of American adults must be desperately bored or lamentably boring in the bedroom. Every month there's a new crop of "secrets" that promise to fan that pitiful, dying ember of decaying romance in your life. Oh, the humanity.

Here's a radical suggestion. Want to know how to make your romantic time great? Talk about it. Ask your mate what feels good. Encourage them to speak up if something is ticklish, or uncomfortable, or just unpleasant. It's not an insult, it's a sign of trust to open up your intimate lives to one another. And whatever you do, float any constructive criticism in oceans of love and praise.

To some extent, the physical act of marriage is like food. Some meals are feasts in the experience and jewels in the memory; some are experiments that don't end up like you thought they would; a lot of meals are simple, familiar things of comfort and sustenance. And very, very occasionally, a meal really doesn't agree with you afterward. That doesn't

[56] Song of Solomon 1:2b

mean you stop eating—you just go back to recipes which work and try again.

Just make it your point to enjoy one another. It's so satisfying to see the excitement, nervousness, and wonder of the honeymoon mature into the comfort, joy, and passion of longtime lovers. The Bible says a lot more about sex than "Yes" here and "No" everywhere else. If you live in the garden where God planted you, you find there is a lot more inside that hedge than you ever expected looking in at the gate. It's all good.

## And that fruitful part?

We always intended to have children, sometime, but really weren't thinking about it in any great detail when we first got married. Yet the connection between sex and childbearing is so obvious and foundational, it really ought to be considered—and embraced—from the very start. Children are a gift from God and should be welcomed, not feared or despised. Being open to conception makes a remarkable difference in the experience of lovemaking—we found it more joyful and intense, when there's no holding back, no worry about something "going wrong."

Unfortunately, we keep meeting couples who are having a silent dialogue at home:

Wife: "I feel like you're using me for your pleasure but you'll blame me if I get pregnant."

Husband: "You hold back when I approach you, and your response makes me feel less of a man."

But the alternative? We'd say the alternative is *wonderful*, but it can feel pretty scary at first. Let's talk about it.

## ~ 7 ~

# How To Have The Right Number of Children

*Behold, children are a heritage from the LORD,*
*The fruit of the womb a reward.*
*Like arrows in the hand of a warrior*
*Are the children of one's youth.*
*Blessed is the man who fills his quiver with them!*
— Psalm 127:3-5 (ESV)

Early in our marriage, we acquired a small orange cat. It took three years to realize he was supposed to be our first son.

Now, we love animals, and we've had long term relationships with dogs, cats, hamsters, and tropical fish throughout our lives. Our families growing up were the archetypical nuclear households, consisting of Dad, Mom, Brother, Sister, Dog and/or Cat. Dog and Cat had different names and for Hal, changed rather frequently, but we always understood the distinction: Doc or Scout or Mac, or Miciona or Sugar or Tribulation (Hal's cat-hating dad suggested the last one) were always pets, not people. Even our widowed grandmother who doted a bit on her poodle never forgot Henretta was just a dog.

But what startled us was learning that Benjamin, our tabby, was our feeble answer to God's leading. It was a year or so into our marriage, we were settled into Hal's first "job" with the Air Force, and we were both taking graduate school classes at night. Somehow, we both started to feel something lacking—like we needed something else living in our home. We already had one cat, and since we had carefully and oh-so-wisely planned our first child for four years into the marriage, we decided it must be time for... another cat.

Later, when we generously allowed God to bless us with a real baby, our eyes were opened. "Oh, that's what the cat was about!" Hal observed. "That was supposed to be our first child."

See, we grew up in towns where nobody had more than two or, at the most, three children. We met a few exceptions, like the old-fashioned Roman Catholic families with eight apiece, or the Mormon family with a houseful, but for all practical purposes, everybody we knew followed the respectable two- or three-child model.

When we were courting, we got around to the question of children eventually. It was evening, we were sitting on a bench by the state capitol on the way to a dinner date, and we were thinking theoretically about marriage and kids and all that. We decided we might go out on a limb and have *four* children, on our own schedule, after we'd enjoyed four years of newlywed bliss together. This was the conversation when we thought marriage should wait until Hal finished his four-year Air Force commitment, not yet begun. Ha.

Well, affection, love, and desire being what they are, we moved the engagement schedule *way* up, and finally had the wedding between Hal's last class in summer school and the actual graduation in August. And while we held to our original schedule for the "correct" time to *start* having children, by the time we had two of them, God had shown us a number of things—including the revelation that our cat could have been our eldest son.

There was lots of love in both our families growing up, and there was never any suggestion that a married couple ought to be childless by choice. We never had any pressure to hurry up and produce grandchildren, either—not even to "preserve the family name," since Hal was the last male descendent of his grandfather Young. It was just assumed that we'd have children eventually, and probably more than one.

But neither was there any suggestion that we should welcome a larger number of kids if God gave them to us. Like most people in our generation, we felt that conceiving and bearing children was so natural and inevitable, we had to put up serious barriers to prevent them. Mary Pride describes a nightmarish image of floating in a little rubber raft, while babies swim up and try to leap into the boat, and frantic not-yet-parents struggle to keep them out.[1] It's allegorical, but that's a common view.

We got another glimpse of the popular institutional viewpoint when our eldest (the human son, not the furry substitute) was ready to apply for college. By that time we had seven, from our 17-year-old senior to a 4-year-old daughter. Much to our surprise, the federal financial aid process said we were poor as dirt. By their standards, a family couldn't live properly with seven children unless they were earning $160,000 a year. Meanwhile, local government officials, aiming to restrict slum-condition housing for immigrant workers, were suggesting outrageous floor space requirements for each person living in a house. We knew from our experience and the lives of many of our friends these were standards of

---

[1] Mary Pride, *All The Way Home: Power For Your Family To Be Its Best* (Westchester, IL: Crossway Books, 1989), p. 29.

luxury or harassment, not an accurate reflection of what it takes to provide for a child.

Yet we run into that mindset all the time. The number of children must be limited to the number of bedrooms. Every child is entitled to a college education and their own car, and girls get a high-ticket wedding, too.

Missing out of the assumptions and the limited discussions we heard was a simple but disturbing question—what does *God* want?

## God means for us to have children

John Murray pointed out that the first passages of Scripture lay a foundation for the rest, and by their announcement to the very first man and woman, have a special meaning which supersedes culture, philosophy, ethnicity and time. He called them "creation mandates" and saw them as the starting point for understanding man's purpose on Earth.

So it's significant that when God created man, the very first commandment recorded in Scripture involves childbearing:

> *So God created man in His own image; in the image of God He created him; male and female He created them. Then God blessed them, and God said to them, "Be fruitful and multiply; fill the earth and subdue it; have dominion over the fish of the sea, over the birds of the air, and over every living thing that moves on the earth."* [2]

---

[2] This reads a little awkwardly in the English translation, but there is more than poetry involved here. Even today in Middle Eastern cultures, a three-fold repetition carries the weight of a legal pronouncement. We see it in many places in Scripture, from real estate transactions (Ephron

There are several things to unpack from this verse, but let's start with the direction, "Be fruitful and multiply." God created Man as male and female, brought them together, and blessed them with the command to go and have children. This is the world before there was sin. God repeated the command to Noah—twice—so it has a role in a fallen world, too.[3]

There are objections that might be raised over applying this verse to modern life; we'll address some of them later. For now, can we agree that when God created marriage, this was part of the program at the very foundation of it? That in the Garden of Eden, God intended marriage to be fruitful?

He says so at the other end of the Old Testament, too. In Malachi chapter 2, the prophet explains why the Lord is rejecting the offerings of Israel:

> *Because the LORD was witness between you and the wife of your youth, to whom you have been faithless, though she is your companion and your wife by covenant.* **Did he not make them one, with a portion of the Spirit in their union? And what was the one God seeking? Godly offspring.** *So guard yourselves in your spirit, and let none of you be faithless to the wife of your youth.*
> — Malachi 2:14-15 (ESV)

---

the Hittite gifted a field to Abraham, saying, "No, my lord, hear me: I give you the field, and I give you the cave that is in it. In the sight of the sons of my people I give it to you."—Genesis 23:11) to the awesome voice of the seraphim crying "Holy, holy, holy is the LORD" (Isaiah 6:3 and Revelation 4:8). In the present passage it seems God is underscoring His sovereignty over humanity: "God created man .. He created him... He created them." Man owes his existence to God, and God reserves the right to give commandments to His creatures.

[3] Genesis 9:1, 7

There are numerous other passages which speak of God's desire to bless His people with children. Psalm 128:3-4 says that the man who fears the Lord *shall* be blessed with a fruitful wife and children around his table. God told Israel repeatedly that when they obeyed His commandments, they would be blessed with children.[4] Even when the entire nation lay in captivity, God's people were told to marry and bear children, and not just to replace themselves, but to multiply:

> *"Thus says the LORD of hosts, the God of Israel, to all the exiles whom I have sent into exile from Jerusalem to Babylon: 'Build houses and live in them; plant gardens and eat their produce.* **Take wives and have sons and daughters; take wives for your sons, and give your daughters in marriage, that they may bear sons and daughters; multiply there, and do not decrease.** *But seek the welfare of the city where I have sent you into exile, and pray to the LORD on its behalf, for in its welfare you will find your welfare.'"*
>
> — Jeremiah 29:4-7 (ESV)

Paul taught that bearing and raising children was a privilege that allowed both men and women to develop and demonstrate their Christian character, and it is a factor to consider before ordaining church officers or approving applications for charity.[5]

As western nations drop below the replacement rate of fertility, and in some countries the average woman undergoes more than six abortions during her childbearing years, the Bible is unmistakable that God does not propose children as

---

[4] Leviticus 26:9, Deuteronomy 6:3; 7:13; 8:1; 13:17; 28:4; 30:16

[5] Regarding elders, Titus 1:6. Regarding deacons, 1 Timothy 3:12. Before approving charity, 1 Timothy 5:4, 10, 14

a threat, a punishment, or a burden. In God's kingdom, children are a gift, and they are a reward which He confers on individual families for His own glory—and for their blessing.

## The Right Number

The more we studied Scripture on the subject, and the more we read from theologians and commentators from previous centuries, the more we were convinced—and convicted—that God's direction for our family did not include a plan for us to take actions to stop bearing children at some pre-determined number. While He could stop giving us children at any time—for God both opens and closes the womb—we realized He should be the judge of that, not we ourselves.

We don't want to fall in the opposite ditch, though. The disciples asked Jesus whether a blind man's sightlessness was due to his own sins or those of his parents. Jesus cut that line of reasoning short and replied, *"It was not that this man sinned, or his parents, but that the works of God might be displayed in him."* [6] It was a matter of God's will, for His own glory. We have numerous friends and acquaintances that never used contraception and only had one or a few children. Sometimes God closes the womb for His own purposes, and we sin if we see the small family or childless couple and we judge them on the presumption that they are turning against God's blessings. The patience of the couple who yearns for children they have not yet borne is a testimony to God's sovereignty, just as much as the diligence of the couple who are striving to raise eight for His glory, knowing a ninth may be in His plans.

For those of us who have followed the culture's view of fertility, though, some re-thinking may be in order. What we

---

[6] John 9:3 (ESV)

discovered was that the whole topic network of the act of marriage, pregnancy, child-bearing, child-nurturing and openness to more children is so connected and so important to the marriage relationship, it is hard to know where to start or how to separate them. What we believe about welcoming the children the Lord sends will affect our feelings toward each other and toward our children in unexpected ways.

Paul uses marriage is an earthly picture of the relationship between Christ, the bridegroom, and the church, His bride. That spiritual relationship is a picture of how husbands and wives should behave toward one another.[7] But Malachi 2:15, as we've seen, points out that childbearing is one of the fundamental purposes of marriage. Because of that, our attitude towards bearing children is foundational to our marriage, despite the echoing silence of the church in this matter in recent years.

We were surprised to find that the church has spoken at length about this topic in the past, even up until the first third of the twentieth century. Contraception is nothing new. Though probably ineffective by today's standards, barrier and chemical contraception, as well as abortion and infanticide, have been around since at least the time of the ancient Egyptians.[8] In response, every mainstream theologian from Christ until the 1930s condemned it.

What changed then? There was a strong movement in western society away from the doctrine of God's special creation toward Darwin's evolution and its ugly stepchildren, eugenics and "family planning." After all, if people *evolved* to this point of human progress, shouldn't we be selecting the

---

[7] Ephesians 5:22-33

[8] Riddle, John M. *Contraception and Abortion from the Ancient World to the Renaissance.* Cambridge, MA: Harvard UP, 1992. 66-68. Print.

best stock possible for reproduction—for the good of the species? That's certainly not a Biblical view, but the church was unable to hold out long against it. The Lambeth Conference of 1930 brought forth a change in the Anglican Church's opposition to contraception, to the allowance that "where there is a morally sound reason for avoiding complete abstinence," artificial methods of birth control would be permissible.[9] Within a couple of decades, the Protestant churches moved en masse from this position of *allowing* contraception to *encouraging* it.

On reflection, has the Christian church grown in holiness since previous centuries, or is in increasingly worldly? Are modern innovations in doctrine improving the church's faithfulness? It pays to think about it.

So what happens if we go back to the older way—trusting God to give us the children He desires for us to have? When we decide to trust God to provide exactly the number of children that we should have—no more, no less—, there comes a wholeheartedness in our physical relationship that is nearly impossible when we are constantly concerned about not conceiving—or worse yet, when we surgically modify our bodies to prevent conception.[10]

## Buts and Whatabouts

The first decision to trust the Lord with family planning is a high hurdle indeed. "How will we feed all those children?" we ask ourselves. "How will take care of them? Will

---

9 Gore, Charles, Bishop of Oxford. "Lambeth on Contraceptives." *Lambeth on Contraceptives*. Project Canterbury: Documenting Anglican History Online, n.d. Web. 27 Aug. 2012. ‹http://anglicanhistory.org/gore/contra1930.html›., originally published 1930.

10 Isn't that the essence of mutilation, to remove or cut a healthy body to interrupt its designed functions?

they get enough attention?" The whole issue is fraught with what-if scenarios.

Seen from the other side of the decision, though, the reality has been far different. Instead of creating a day care bus with twenty 3-year-olds—Hal's particular nightmare—, God gave us a family of individuals, spaced at manageable intervals. Each of them bears our family resemblance, but in different mixtures, so that each has his or her own personality. And each of our eight children has added so much to our family life that we can't imagine living without any one of them.

The longer period of childbearing opens new vistas to parenting. The sheer joy of having a baby at age 45, when you have already seen your first child grow to adulthood, is remarkable. We enjoyed the last two babies so much more, knowing how fleeting childhood is and how delightful it is to watch your own progeny grow and mature and learn to serve God. We often lay in bed in the morning and just laughed and played with the baby. So few people our age have that experience—they don't know what they are missing!

We've found too that our thinking and outlook have stayed optimistic and even playful long after some of our friends became jaded. We've been treated again and again to the wonder of a young child discovering the sky overhead, learning to read, or awakening to the spiritual side of life, reminding us of the freshness of God's grace and provision.

On the other hand, some of us are making long term trades that haven't been thought through. Melanie was sitting at a children's party once when we had just three young children. Another mother was shocked that we'd had another baby.

"We just can't afford it!" she said. "We couldn't have bought that new van out there if we'd had another child."

Melanie, stunned, said, "Would you trade your sweet daughter over there for a van?"

"Of course not!" the other mother said, horrified.

"But isn't that just what you said? You wanted to buy a van more than you wanted another child?"

Melanie was younger and more brash then, and she probably didn't make any friends that day. On the other hand, though, she was right. People all around us are fighting conception because they want to freely seek their own pleasures. How Satan has deceived them! The joy we have in our children is one of the chief pleasures of life, one the Lord even gives to the unbeliever, and to a degree, to the animals. How sad, how ironic, that people would give up one of the deepest and long-lasting pleasures of earthly life in a quest for vague and fleeting self-indulgence.

It's a fact that joy is sometimes mixed with hardship, and that may complicate the decision and hamper our trust. Our first son was born five weeks early; our second *nearly* came ten weeks too soon. That was when we discovered Melanie has an incompetent cervix which requires surgery in the early weeks of pregnancy and extended bed rest to enable her to carry a child to term. Coupled with that, she is prone to preterm labor, and incidentally, a tendency to develop gestational diabetes—further distractions which add to the challenge. From a human standpoint, each successive pregnancy has been a slowly-wrecking train that involves the entire family.

Why continue? Because the Bible tells us, and our experience attests, those children are a huge blessing. God has given them to us as a reward. By His grace, they're an *eternal* blessing as well. How can you compare an uncomfortable, sometimes frightening, nine months with an eternal life?

What's more, the challenges we experience during Melanie's pregnancies have motivated us all to become more mature and organized. The enforced rest ensures that Melanie slows down and spends extra time with the younger children before the birth of their new sibling. All of the children are encouraged to become footservants and handmaidens to their mother—how's that for honor?—and each of them learn new skills out of simple necessity.

Another unexpected blessing of our large family has been our older children's delight in each pregnancy. With all the work and worry that come along with them, what would you expect our children's reactions to be to the announcements? To our surprise (and relief), they are always thrilled, literally jumping with joy! Yes, they know it will be hard work, but they also know how sweet a new baby is, how entertaining a toddler can be, how much fun it is to have someone else to share our good times with.

We used to worry whether our children would get enough attention, or if they would resent us having a large family. What we failed to take into account is that although a child who is one of eight doesn't have as much individual time with each parent, they also have seven additional members of their immediate family to talk with, play with, or love.[11]

---

[11] Ostensibly, there's less parental time when divided by eight instead of two. However, we'd question whether the family with two children is really spending as much time with them as the parents might think.

What's more, the interplay of viewpoints and personalities, all different though closely related, provides an endless variety of ideas, jokes, questions, and answers. When we visit our family's tiny vacation place at the lake, we may sleep on the floor for lack of nine beds, but the evenings are full of charades, board games, and reading aloud. We laugh and enjoy the fellowship just like a party with our friends. Having a large family makes nearly everything (except laundry) more entertaining.

When we were new parents, Melanie was treated to a baby shower at our church (since John arrived early, the shower came late). Among all the advice offered was a warning to never let your baby sleep in your bed. "You'll never get them out again," one of the older ladies said, with nods of agreement all around. "And you might roll over on them in the night." The nods continued.

But lo and behold, as soon as the advice group broke up and mixed into the rest of the guests, several of the very same women sidled up to Melanie and whispered, "You know, I took my babies to bed with me. They seemed to sleep better, and so did I."

That was an important lesson, and one we've seen repeated many times—not the advisability of different sleeping arrangements, but the difference between the party line and the real story. Everyone knew the popular wisdom called for keeping babies in their bassinet or crib, so everyone gave public assent to the litany of advice. The reality was completely opposite, and when the coast was clear, people told Melanie the truth.

In the matter of children, there is an unspoken agreement to uphold the received dogma of society. We heard it about pregnancy, birth control, childbirth, breastfeeding, and discipline, and the list goes on. We were told publicly on many occasions about the dangers of large families, but always someone would tell us privately, "I was one of nine children myself, and we never lacked someone to play with or something to do. I wonder if kids today have as much fun as we did?" Our advice is to listen to what people tell you, but don't accept their first statements at face value; often there's a follow up to let you know the inside story is quite different.

## And how do you get here?

Opening your home to more children has an impact on your marriage, no question. Right at the outset, you have to reach agreement with each other, seeking to avoid conflict, blame and resentment later on when you should be experiencing joy. While that's true of any life decision, a negative response that involves the life of a child and the physical closeness of your marriage can cut very deeply. It's crucial to line up your hearts first.

Frequently, it seems, the mother is the first to desire more children, as the one who is most tuned in to young children emotionally. Often Dad is hesitant, worrying over provision—how can he support more children financially? That's a natural concern, though it should be remembered and believed that all our provision comes from God, not solely by our efforts, and that He has promised to provide for our needs. We've found that children are not nearly as expensive to raise as the world seems to think. If you want evidence, take a look at the floor plans of homes built in the early- to mid-20th Century, when families averaged several more children than today and households often included an elderly relative or two. The older houses are more compact, rooms are smaller, and there is less space devoted to impressing the neighbors—fewer formal rooms and grand entryways. There is less square footage devoted to luxuries like giant bathrooms and walk-in closets, and more real living space. We found our boys, growing up with bunk beds, actually preferred a crowded bedroom so they could minimize sleeping space in exchange for playrooms and work- or hobby areas elsewhere in the house.

College costs are often a concern. The tendency to raise credential thresholds is a problem in our economy, where jobs which once were open to high school graduates are now closed to those with less than an associate's degree. Yet we've found that financial aid is available to students with a decent academic record and an interesting resume, so long as you remain flexible about where and how you attend. If you set your sights on sending every child to your alma mater, come what may, you may be painting yourself into a corner down the road. Our experience so far has been that every child has different gifts and callings which tend to guide them to different educational institutions, and God is providing means to gain that education—not necessarily at our own colleges, but at schools more appropriate for our children's needs.

What we have to remember, though, is:

> I have been young, and now am old, yet I have not seen the righteous forsaken or his children begging for bread.[12]

Whichever mate is wishing for more children, we recommend discussing it openly as your heart's desire, careful to avoid criticism or recrimination. Try reading some books together to investigate the idea; we read a number of authors

---

[12] Psalm 37:25

from different perspectives before we reached agreement. At that point, it's time to shut up and pray! God holds each of our hearts in His hand, and we have seen many, many hearts changed in this area through gentle sharing and serious prayer.

Once you are in agreement, though, it brings a freedom and joy to your love life that is remarkable. We probably shouldn't be surprised; if procreation is one of the major purposes of the marriage bed and of marriage itself, why should we marvel that avoiding childbearing would have a negative impact? Couples tell us that when they made the decision to welcome whatever issue the Lord would bring to their relationship, they felt like they had truly given themselves to their mate for the first time. It's sad to realize the hesitation they had accepted in their relationship up to that point, but exciting too, for those contemplating this step.

## The Changing Schedule

When you open your marriage to children, it becomes more important to understand how the cycles of childbearing can affect your life. After all, you are likely to go through more of them! That is not always the case, of course; we know several couples who have never used birth control and only had one child in decades of married life. Most of us, though, are likely to have more children than the norm, so we need to go about our childbearing with wisdom and thoughtfulness, planning for the long haul.

For some of us, pregnancy will mean careful preparation. With Melanie's health issues, we always invested time in cooking ahead and stocking the freezer, deep-cleaning the house, battening down for what feels like an impending storm. Other may face a swamp of depression after the baby comes, and they may need to seek out help and medication in advance to deal with it. *All* of us will face the exhaustion of pregnancy and the increased work and fatigue a new baby brings. If we know that's coming, you can think through what needs to happen and do as much in advance as possible.

We've found it's also important to welcome the challenges as opportunities for our whole family to grow in Christ. For example, during our bedrest pregnancies, Melanie has to practice patience and learn to control her increasing emotionalism. Hal has to work harder than usual and control his anxiety for Melanie and the baby. The children have to work harder, too, and be more mature and responsible. It's good for all of us, and God is good to allow us to go through it: at the end is a happy reward, a new little life added to our home! And Lord could teach patience, diligence, and self-control in many ways without an earthly joy arriving so quickly at the end.

## Preparing for Delivery

We were convinced of the desirability of a natural childbirth, avoiding surgery and unneeded procedures as much as possible, from the very beginning. Beside the documented risks of a caesarian section, it is increasingly hard to find a medical provider who will allow a vaginal birth after caesarian (V-BAC). Some doctors are hesitant to even accept a patient with multiple c-sections in her history already. That alone would be motivation enough to do all that you can to avoid a c-section, but the things you do to prepare for a natural birth are also likely to be good for your marriage relationship. Even the birth itself can be a time for drawing closer as a couple. Melanie has found that when she relies on the Lord and on Hal to get her through the difficulties of labor, she feels enormous affection for both when she's safely through!

Probably the advice which has helped us the most through labor has been understanding the emotional signposts of labor as described in *Natural Childbirth, The Bradley Way*[13] (be aware many would find the pictures in this book inappropriate for Dad). When a mom first goes into labor, she usually feels excited: "The day is finally here! I get to hold my baby!" and that's when everyone pictures heading to the hospital (or wherever you plan to deliver). It's way too soon, though, because there may be hours of comparatively easy labor that would be much easier to handle at home, where you can walk around, find distraction, and eat what you want. This excited time marks the stage of early labor—usually from 0-3 cm dilated. We once heard that if you can smile for the "leaving for the hospital" photo, go back inside!

On the other hand, when a mother is in active labor, she is very serious. It takes concentration to get through the hard contractions of this stage, and she won't brook any messing around. When mom responds to the picture-taking with snarling "Get. In. The. Car. NOW." or "Get the midwife here right now!", it's time to prepare for the birth and get ready for the baby to come. This stage is when the cervix is opening from 3-7 cm and gets increasingly challenging to bear. During this time, the husband can show his love for his wife by taking tender care of her: helping her get settled in where she'll give birth, bringing her ice water, rubbing her back, getting a cold wash cloth for her face and a hot one for her pelvis. This is a very special time when the wife feels very vulnerable and often has a hard time thinking clearly. The husband can protect her by running interference with any medical helpers they have, and he is uniquely equipped to encourage her and care for her as he looks after her comfort, prays for her and even sings to her.

---

[13] McCutcheon, S., and E. Ingraham. *Natural Childbirth the Bradley Way.* Plume Books, 1996. Print.

The signpost which is most easily misunderstood is the panic that sets in with the transition phase. This occurs as the cervix completes its opening in preparation for the birth, from 7 to 10 cm. The panic is caused by the increasingly long and powerful contractions *as well as* the physical and hormonal transition from labor to pushing. What's sad is that this is when most moms ask for medication because they feel they "just can't do this for hours!" when really they may be within a few minutes of the end. Administering medication at this point is so late in the process it usually won't take effect until after the pushing begins, and then it interferes with the mother's ability to cooperate with her body. This is the perfect time for the prepared husband to jump in and say, "Honey! You are panicking. You're in transition! That means the baby is almost here!" The mom will feel relieved and buckle down to the job.

Having this knowledge of normal, predictable emotional changes can help a couple make the right decisions during childbirth, and generally, the husband will need to take the lead because of his wife's understandable distraction.

Another point to remember, Dad, is that while labor goes through these predictable stages, it may go fast, slow, or at a changeable rate. Sometimes a mother will hit the panic of transition, then despair when the nurse finds she's only at 5 cm instead of 10 cm. That can change in as little as 20 minutes, though the mother may be convinced she still has hours of labor to endure. This is why the visible, outward emotional signpoints are so important to remember.

The signposts repeat themselves once the pushing begins—initial excitement, followed by serious attention to work, and then panic right before the end. Knowing that this is normal, with an on-his-toes husband right at hand to give support and perspective, can make birth a time of joy and increased unity in marriage. Why should the relieved mother plant a kiss on the obstetrical resident, when her husband is the one who has stood by her and helped bring her through the whole event?

## When the Plan Doesn't Work Out

Sometimes this pattern just doesn't come together. Maybe the mother hasn't been told all these things, or she doesn't get the support she needs. Sometimes her doctor doesn't support natural childbirth or he's impatient or even makes a mistake. It could be there's something physical in mom or baby that calls for intervention, conditions such as placenta previa, pre-eclampsia, or incompetent cervix. When it's necessary, medical intervention can be life-saving.

Someone was fussing at us for accepting a surgical cerclage to manage Melanie's incompetent cervix. Our friend, a strong proponent of minimal intervention in pregnancy, challenged us, "Well, what do you think women did hundreds of years ago?" Melanie answered, "Sadly, they got pregnant again and again, only to lose every baby sometime in mid-pregnancy. I'm glad I didn't live back then." There is no reason to apologize when you need an intervention. Pastor John Piper, a cancer survivor, wrote that God heals by miracle and by medicine; it's a good thing God has blessed us with knowledge that can keep mom and baby safe in those circumstances now.

It's harder to accept interventions, though, when you've received treatments you didn't want or didn't need. Sometimes, even if you did need medical intervention, your plans for a wonderful birth were derailed and you're left feeling grief, anger, sometimes even pain, during a time which should be one of the happiest of your life. It can be really difficult. Many times Melanie has laid in the bed wondering why it had to be so hard for us to have babies when her expectant friends were out gardening or playing tennis. We have to remember that discovering a medical need does not mean we're failures or somehow lower our worth. We live in a fallen world and because of that, things often just don't work right. We can't understand why God allows us to go through difficult times, but we have to trust that He knows best; that he's accomplishing some purpose for our good and for His glory, and that we'll understand some day.

We have friends who lived through an incredible trial. A doctor's error after their daughter was born has caused her a great deal of suffering, many hospitalizations, and ongoing consequences. Yet, they've been an example to us in their forgiveness of the hospital staff and their lack of bitterness. We wonder if we could do the same. How brightly their testimonies have shined in that fire! We don't think anyone could ever doubt they were really Christians; only God can give you strength to bear such a burden with grace.

So, what do you do if things just didn't go like you'd hoped? You forgive (with God's help), heal (with God's help), and see if there's anything you can do to make things better next time. You love your baby. You cling tight to the Lord. He is faithful and He will help you. We've needed that help and we've experienced it ourselves.

## After the Baby's Here

A natural birth like we described allows the best chance for the new family to enjoy getting to know one another without distraction. The natural endorphins released in labor usually leave the mother feeling excited and happy, and without the side effects of anesthesia or surgery. Regardless of your birth story, though, you have, with the help of the Lord, brought forth a new life. It is an incredible joy to hold the living, physical expression of your love for one another. Like the discoveries of early marriage, there are so many things we don't really understand very well until we have our own children.

The weeks after childbirth are another time that the husband's love and tenderness will always be appreciated. It seriously takes about six weeks for a mother to recover from childbirth, even if she has an easy, short labor, because of all the changes in her body that accompany birth. It's a time that moms need extra rest and care. A father's tender care for his wife and baby during this time will say worlds to her and to their children.

In addition to the benefits of natural childbirth, we've been thoroughly pleased with the results of natural child nourishment too—breastfeeding from the start. It really makes sense to use the preparation time to do everything you can to get nursing off to a good start. Very, very few women have a physical problem that prevents them from producing a full milk supply, but many women will have some initial difficulties and need help in the early days. In earlier centuries, a young woman would come to the birth of her first child having seen many babies nursed—her mother's, her sister's, her aunt's—and she would know how to hold a baby, how to get a baby to latch on. When her own baby arrived, if she had questions, these experiences moms were available to help her out. These days, though, a mom can come to birth having never seen a baby nurse, and her mother may be just as uncertain!

It's important to read ahead and to get support lined up. Why? Mother's milk is the food God designed for babies. If the mother is unable to get the help she needs, or in the rare event of a physical problem, we're glad there's formula to help, but breastfeeding provides lifelong health benefits for both the mother and baby in ways formulas can't. Babies who receive mother's milk have lower cholesterol,[14] lower incidence of diabetes,[15] fewer cases of asthma,[16] and protection against some childhood cancers.[17] Mothers who nurse their babies have fewer breast, ovarian, and cervical cancers, better bone density,[18] and less chance of developing diabetes themselves.[19]

Some of this may seem fantastic if you've never heard it before. When we were still early in our marriage, a friend loaned Melanie a book on breastfeeding which referenced many of these benefits. Melanie read some of these passages to Hal, who was not opposed in principle to breastfeeding, but still thought this was too good to be true. May prevent cancer and diabetes? Helps control cholesterol? *Honestly, this sounds like a pitch for patent medicines*, he thought.

But as we both read the results of many controlled studies and realized these were documentable facts, it began to dawn on us. This only seemed "too good to be true" because our expectations were so low. What if God created mothers and babies, and designed a nutritional system that was clean, portable, and fresh; that helped jump start the baby's immune system and provide a foundation for other key processes in the baby's body; and would adjust itself to the baby's needs in quantity and content—all of which breastfeeding is and

[14] Riordan, Jan and Karen Wambach, *Breastfeeding and Human Lactation*, Fourth Edition (Sudbury, MA: Jones and Bartlett Publishers, 2010) p.126

[15] Riordan, p. 138

[16] Riordan, p.140

[17] Riordan, p.138

[18] Riordan, p.519

[19] Riordan, p.520

does. Then if we developed a substitute which would be filling and provide basic nourishment, the most obvious need of the moment, would we be reasonable to expect that formula to do all the other complex internal things which mother's milk was made to do? Or would we be prone to settle on the man-made product (easy to produce in a factory setting, ship and store for retail convenience, and be simple to market) and think we'd duplicated "nature"?

Hmmm.

Please don't think that we're slamming you if you weren't able to nurse your babies. Melanie has been a lactation consultant for over ten years and a *La Leche League* leader for over twenty. She's seen so many moms who didn't get the support they need, got bad advice, or just got overwhelmed. One doctor in our area recommended a mom wean her baby because she needed a basic antibiotic—a perfectly safe medication to take while nursing. It was a completely unnecessary grief to that young mom. Melanie's seen other moms who had a physical inability to produce enough milk, such as mothers with hypoplastic breasts. If you haven't been able to nurse your babies, don't beat yourself up. If you're still bearing children and your difficulty was one that can be overcome, then maybe you can find better help and try again next time. One of our friends breastfed for the first time with her fourth child. And if you're beyond that stage of life, maybe you can make sure your daughters and daughters-in-law get plenty of help and love when they have new babies.

## The Fertility Effect

There's another effect of breastfeeding, which circles back to the subject of this chapter. If a mother is nursing a baby as it seems God intended, it delays the return of fertility.[20] Now, understand us here, we do believe that children are a gift from the Lord and to be rejoiced in no matter how close together they come, but this natural infertility is part of God's design which allows us, in most cases, to have time to care for each of our young children as they need us. The longer the baby nurses, the longer it tends to be until the mother's fertility returns. It's a beautiful balance God created, and if you do any family history, you can probably see it in your own ancestor's households—six or eight or twelve children, neatly spaced at two year intervals.

Don't be discouraged, though, if fertility returns sooner than you were expecting. We had a friend many years ago who was frantic that she had a baby every year without a break. When we met her she had four young children, and told us she had questioned God and wondered if they had done the right thing not to use birth control. Shortly after their fourth child was born, she went through menopause—in her early thirties! She said afterward she was so thankful the Lord had given her all those children in a row—the only children she'd ever have!

We know families who have 12 or 14 children and those who've never used birth control who have one. The goal is not to have as many children as possible—if that were God's purpose, He likely would have given Adam more than one wife and not built the natural child-spacing effect into breastfeeding. Rather, our goal is to welcome all the children

---

20 Riordan p. 707

the Lord is pleased to give our family. We are so thankful for each of ours!

Our youngest child was born when Melanie was 45 years old. We had so many negative remarks like "How will you keep up with a toddler?" (It keeps you young, we discovered.) It's been an utter joy, though. She has brought so much delight and pleasure to our house. It's so much more fun having a toddler around when you know how brief that period is, when you know how quickly you'll be packing them off to college.

The funny thing is, we think most people know that at heart already. Melanie noticed years ago that the initial response to our large family from her sisters in Christ was, "Better you than me!" When Melanie responded with how much she loved her family and how thankful she was to God for them, often they quietly expressed regret, "I've always wished we'd had more children," but explained they'd had their tubes tied or their husbands had had a vasectomy. Those are sometimes reversible, but it's an expensive and not-always-successful procedure. It's sad to us that many of these couples had never heard anyone question the party line before they were sterilized. It's seems like everyone is doing it, most are regretting it, but no one is talking about it. It's hardly fair to the next generation to come along.

We understand this is very controversial and there are some who will want to slam this book closed right about now. Please don't. Skip ahead if you must, but we urge you to take a look at the facts first, and then pray about whether the Lord wants to bring more blessings into your family. You won't regret it.

Just recently, all the boys were home and we were in the van together traveling to a family reunion. One of the guys suggested we sing to pass the time, another called out, "Come Thou Fount of Every Blessing" and we all began to sing that old favorite.

It was the congregational hymn at our wedding. We clearly remember singing it together at the front of the church hearing nothing but each other, the congregation only background music. Now, our two voices were joined by little girls' voices singing in their high trebles, the boys' voices sounding loudly beside them, and our grown sons singing harmony around us. The tide of music swelled and surrounded, and tears came into our eyes. God had taken our two voices, lifted together in praise to Him, joyfully blending together, and had raised up a choir around us— a choir of voices like ours, but different, voices with characteristics of both of us—something from us, and like us, but more. He multiplied the praise to Himself by giving us these children. The joy nearly burst our hearts.

Just wait until the grandchildren come!

*Then God blessed them, and God said to them,*
**"...have dominion**
*over the fish of the sea, over the birds of the air,*
*and over every living thing that moves on the earth."*

— Genesis 1:28b

# ~ 8 ~

## Money — Yours, Mine or Ours?

*For where your treasure is, there your heart will be also.*

— Matthew 6:21

Some time ago we read a comment from a woman who had lived with her boyfriend for several years and had two children by him, but complained she couldn't trust him to handle a shared bank account.

So, you share one bed, parent the same children, live in the same house, but want to keep separate checkbooks? What's going on here?

The Holmes and Rahe Stress Scale is a list of life events which can cause health-effecting levels of stress. Studies done with large populations, different income groups, and even different cultures, confirmed the initial results of the American study by Thomas Holmes and Richard Rahe. The most stressful life event is the death of a spouse; the Test ranks this as 100. Some are joyful, like the birth of a child, a big job promotion, or the marriage of a child; some are disasters like the loss of a job, a major illness, or a jail term. "Change in financial state" ranks in 16th place, yet nearly all of events 1 through 15 will have an impact on our finances.

Money is a source of great stress at some time or other in every marriage we know of. Every family will likely face a time of financial trouble or windfall or conflict. It's just life. It doesn't seem like finances should be that different from the rest of the stresses in our life, yet most counselors agree that fights over finances are a major factor in divorces. What is the best way to navigate through these dangerous rapids in our relationship? How can you handle this aspect of marriage in a way that glorifies God and builds unity? We believe the first step is to get married—with everything you have! If the two shall become one flesh, how can they remain two pocketbooks? It's becoming more and more popular for couples to enter marriage with the attitude of *your money* versus my money. This is easier to maintain when both parties are working, there's more than enough money to go around to satisfy even two self-indulgent married/no children twenty-somethings, but what happens when the children come, or sickness, or job loss? Is the spouse who's suddenly not earning now relegated to child status, "Honey, may I please have some money for an allowance?" That's not very good for your relationship!

Just like in conflict, holding back from unity, "just in case" it doesn't work out. It doesn't help at all, but creates its own disunities. If you are holding back from merging your finances for fear you'll face a divorce and end up penniless, we believe you are making divorce much more likely. This is the kind of thinking you go through, "We need to make a big purchase. I hope I can get him to spend his money for it!" You are refusing to invest, this time quite literally, in the relationship and so things around you become a tangible, visible expression of your lack of unity!

"Don't eat on my couch! You might drop something on it!"

"Hey, be careful with my camera!"

And so with every purchase, you are drawn farther and farther apart and continually reminded that you are not fully one. This is **not** the way it's supposed to be, or the way that it has been in our cultural history. The traditional wedding vows stated, "...with all my worldly goods I thee endow."[1]

## And the Two Shall Become One... Account

If you're going to vow to love and honor someone "as long as you both shall live," then you ought to truly become one flesh—and join your finances, too. After all, that's about the fleshiest part of most of us! That's where we really see what's important to us:

"Of course, I will share my innermost being with you and make love to you! What? But, that's my nest egg you are talking about! Are you crazy?"

"Oh honey, of course I'll love you even when you are old and gray. I love you just as you are! I think you're gorgeous! What? No way am I paying off your school loans! Do you realize how hard I worked in college to stay out of debt?"

When we marry, we take on the other person's finances, good, bad or indebted, as our own. That's tough, but it's truth. That's the way your creditors will see it, and that's the way you ought to see it. After all, if even our bodies belong to each other, surely our money does. When you consider that everything you own, you own jointly, from your pots and pans to your bank accounts, it changes your attitudes.

[1] "Book of Common Prayer." in Barlett, John. *Familiar Quotations, 10th Ed.*, 1919. Bartleby Great Books Online. N.d. Web. 29 Aug. 2012. ‹http://www.bartleby.com/100/775.html

When everything belongs to the family, then first of all, you learn to share. That's really hard when you've worked hard for something and you fear the other person won't care for it like you do. Hal had to battle with himself over this with regards to his camera equipment when we were first married. It had been something he'd collected and cherished and been proud of. It was difficult to see Melanie casually say, "Hey, hand me the camera." The really neat thing about it is that Melanie had no idea! She didn't find out until years later that this had even been an internal struggle for Hal. He'd just conquered it, and done the right thing.

It's an important lesson in putting people before things and especially putting one particular person above your own wants and desires. Does that mean you can't even speak up if say, your new wife wants to put your 20 year old stamp collection in the yard sale? No! Certainly not, but it's all in how you say it. If you yell out, "Hey that's mine! Get your hands off of it!" you're tearing at the fabric of your marriage. However, if you take that opportunity to share why you love those stamps, "Hey, let's not sell those, let me tell you about them..." - the precious memories of your young boyhood, the dreams you had, what you were like back then, she'll never be able to put them in the yard sale, not even after you've gone home to heaven!

## One Income... One Heart

It was pretty frightening thinking about Hal's income being our only income once we were married. Melanie was a little afraid that she would feel like a child, with no independence to make decisions involving money. Hal soon put her heart at ease. He's always stood by the principle that everyone contributes to the family, not just the one working for a living. That means when Hal was working for a salary (we have our own business now), it was our salary. How does that work in day to day life? We have to come to some kind of agreement about how we want our money to be spent. We need to have principles to base our decisions on. Some of ours have been:

We will tithe.
We will pay off credit card balances every month, not go into credit card debt.
We will save for emergencies.
We need to be in thorough agreement for big purchases.

Does that mean we've never failed to pay a tithe, or have never let a credit card balance go on far too long or failed to save for a time? Certainly not! We're not perfect, by any stretch of the imagination. In fact, the past several years of medical crises and economic slowdown have forced us to make many financial decisions that have grieved us, but those guiding principles, as well as our others, have kept us going in the right general direction for decades now. That's how we make decisions and we seldom disagree on expenditures because we are both using the same parameters for those decisions.

Sometimes the principles are not super clear, though. What's a big purchase? For some few couples, it might be $5000. For us, it has ranged from $150 to as little as $10 when money has been critically tight. It's the amount that is not in the budget and would strain the budget. Our rule is, if it makes a difference ask. And that's not even inviolable. One morning, one of our sons called from Edinburgh. He was sharing how he'd been visiting all the Covenanters' sites and thinking about the martyrs and the brave men who'd been our forefathers in the faith. He shared, as an aside, that it was a shame his budget was so tight or he'd buy himself a kilt kit in our family tartan. He just didn't feel comfortable spending that much when he might run out of money before he got home. Melanie thought about it and remembered the loden wool coats she and Hal had bought years ago traveling through Europe. It had been hard to justify the expenditure, but every time they'd seen those coats in the 23 years since they'd thought happily of their adventure. "We'll cover it, son, as your Christmas and birthday and graduation next year!" "But Mom, you guys don't have the money, do you?" "We'll find it. Remember our loden wool coats?" So far so good, until Melanie forgot to mention it to Hal and John called Daddy to thank him! Thankfully, Hal didn't blow a gasket, but just waited until they could talk about it. And when they did, they were in complete agreement. It comes from having the same principles and being like-minded.

## Your Financial Assistant

The easiest way to make this work is with a budget. A budget isn't a strait jacket, meant to take all the joy out of our life, or a policeman to follow you around and keep you from spending what you want to. Instead, it makes sure you spend your money as you want by allowing you to decide how to spend it when you have all the information in front of you and not the temptation. This allows the two of you to discuss your priorities and figure out your goals and principles in a way that doesn't embarrass anyone ("Hon-ey! We can't afford this!") or inspire regrets ("We really blew it and now we can't pay our credit card bill."). For many of us, this is going to mean some serious growing up! We highly recommend going through a Biblical financial training program such as Dave Ramsey's "Financial Peace University"[2] to help you work out what you believe and how to turn those beliefs into action.

---

[2] For more information, see the website http://www.daveramsey.com/fpu/

## Mama, the Accountant, or Dad, the CFO?

Some families believe that the Biblical order of the family requires that Dad be in charge of the finances. We disagree. Keeping track of the money is a task, using tools, and doesn't set policy. Policy needs to be set by the couple together with the husband having the final say as a part of his leadership. That has nothing to do with keeping track of it. The accounts need to be kept by the person most able to keep them, in love. If one of you is really good at tracking down the last penny and the other thinks balancing within a hundred dollars or so is good enough, guess which should keep the finances? This is a balancing act, though, because it is very tempting for the accountant in the family to call their poor happy-go-lucky spouse on the carpet like a little child with caught with their hand in the cookie jar. "What in the world did you spend $33.48 for at Office Max on July 8th? Why didn't you turn in a receipt? How am I supposed to track our finances if you won't be responsible?" Uh-uh. Can't do it. You've got to treat each other with gentleness and respect, especially if one of you is asking for answers.

## Hard Times are Hard

It's really hard to show each other that gentleness and respect when times get really hard. It's tempting for a wife to offer her husband critical advice when he's lost a job - don't do this, ladies! He desperately needs you to believe in him to have the confidence he needs to find a new job. Or for a husband to try to force his wife into leaving the children with someone else and getting a job when he is afraid they won't be able to pay their bills. Instead, work together to find a solution that keeps your family principles intact and has the least negative impact on your family dynamics.

When times get really tight, we need to keep a tight hold on our tongues! Stress makes it much harder to keep our self-control and this is an area we can hurt each other so badly in. Often in times of stress, we are so harried we make mistakes, sometimes huge ones. Melanie is a fanatic about paying bills on time, so it was a bit of shock when she completely forgot there were even bills to pay when our newborn was in the hospital with a life-threatening condition. When the "You haven't paid your bill" letter came, both of us about had a heart attack. It would have been too easy to start throwing around accusations, but we still had a bill to pay—and a sick child to take care of!

Likewise, when crises come, sometimes even the best laid financial plans are chucked aside. Melanie remembers that when Hal had stage IV cancer, suddenly her commitment to a balanced budget and careful spending didn't seem important at all. We were in complete survival mode, doing everything we could to keep the family and business going and help Hal to survive the cancer. We ate out too much, spent too much, plus had a lot of extra bills that couldn't be helped. We are still paying for that time. It happens.

Commit to living through those financial disasters which come to most couples sooner or later without recriminations and blame. Remember, that when two walk together, they can pick each other up.

## Yours, Mine, Ours, or His?

Of course, the very best attitude to have about your finances is to remember that none of it belongs to you at all. The entire world and everything in it belongs to God. When we ask ourselves, "How does God want us to spend His money?" it sure changes things. It becomes a sacred trust to decide where the money goes. Likewise, when we think, "How in the world can we pay for what we have to have," it helps a lot to remember that if we really need it, God will provide it.

Our favorite example of this happened during that super stressful year when Hal was fighting cancer. The oncologist had encouraged us to drive to the conventions where we were speaking as much as possible to avoid the exposure to germs Hal would get if we flew (all those people in a tight space with recirculating air). We were headed out on a tour of the Midwest to speak and our mothers were worried sick. To be fair, our old van *had* been towed six times in the last year. And, the air conditioner had died a long and painful death. But, it was an April trip and more to the point, it was the only thing we had.

Hal's mom called, "Could you check to see how much it would take to rent a van for the trip." Way too much was the answer.

Melanie's mom mentioned every 15-passenger van for sale in the county, never seeming to hear us when we said, "Mom, we just don't have the money!" Finally, Melanie lost it one day, "Mom, if the Lord wants us to have a new van, He's going to have to *give* us one! We just can't afford it."

Three days later, a family in our homeschool support group called. "We just realized that we've both been secretly thinking the same thing. We believe the Lord wants you to have our van." Hal couldn't believe it at first, thinking our friends wanted to sell us the van and remember, we didn't have the money to buy one. They soon set us straight. All they would take is $500 to replace what they'd paid to get it into peak condition. Their van was seven years newer than the one we were replacing! The title was transferred the night before we left on the Midwest trip.

Most blessedly, it not only had air conditioning, but it was super-cool. To this day, over three years later, whenever we get into the van all hot and tired, the children sing out, "God bless the Steinackers!" when the air comes on.

God is able not only to provide reliable transportation, but to bless us with air conditioning, too, even when we can't afford it.

Recognizing God's ownership is a huge help when things go expensively wrong, too. As we write, we're waiting on a fax with an estimate to repair someone's car. When we look at our finances, it's pretty stressful waiting - there is no extra money right now - and we know how bad it can get.

Take last year. Please. The spark plugs blew out one afternoon when we were shopping in the big city near us. It was a pretty expensive repair by our standards, some $1200, so we were shocked when just a few weeks later, it happened again to the other side. It was such a rotten time, too. Hal had driven the older boys and their friends to a neighboring state for a special Christian concert. What a mess! We had to repair it, though, it was cheaper than buying another. The third time it happened, our mechanic recommended we replace the engine. Ow! Now we were paying $5000 or more for a new engine and we sure didn't expect that.

As we were getting ready to leave on a speaking trip all the way across the country, we took our "what amounts to a new van"[3] to the shop to get the tires aligned. Uh oh! The

---

[3] In James Herriot's books, whenever his boss Siegfried had the car repaired, he'd take James out to look at it and lecture him on how to

ball joints were shot. It would **not** be safe to drive across the Rockies. And the Rockies were between us and our commitments! Thankfully, Melanie's brother surprised us by paying for most of it.

We took off across the country in our now, surely, good-as-new van. We made it to Oklahoma before the breakdown —and we were supposed to speak that night. The fantastic folks at the shop we found heroically searched all over town for the right hose and raced to finish it in time for us to make our engagement with fifteen minutes to spare. Whew!

The corker came when we, exhausted after a long day sightseeing in Muir Woods and San Francisco, pulled into the campground at the top of Mount Madonna outside Gilroy, California. We made the complete circle looking for the perfect camping spot under the redwood trees. "Uh oh!" we noticed as we reached the beginning again, "Somebody's leaking red... That's us!" Yes, the transmission died on top of a mountain on the other end of the continent from home. Unbelievable.

Why on earth didn't we just buy another van when this first happened? It would have made a lot more sense! We ended up spending probably twice what we would have on a comparable used van. We just didn't know! Each expenditure made sense at the time with what we knew. Why, though, did the Lord allow all that to happen? It messed up our finances terribly and seemed so unnecessary. We don't know. We do know, though, that He is sovereign and all our money belongs to Him, anyway. If He wants to spend it on mechanics from coast to coast (literally!), well, that is His privilege. He really does know best.

---

care for it, intoning, "You have here what amounts to a new car."

We saw lots of bright spots of His love and provision in all this, too. The van on top of the mountain late at night? It broke down right in front of one of the only unoccupied camping spots! We just set up camp right there. The Lord provided kind new friends to help us along to the next convention and got the transmission fixed before we had to move on to the next speaking engagement.

It seems hard after struggling so much with health issues and having so little money to spare to face a series of events like that with the van. When we remember, though, our Lord's ownership of our assets, we can relax. If the Lord chooses to spend his money that way, then we can trust him to provide for our other needs. The looser the grasp you have of your funds in this way, the less stressful managing them will be.

Why is money such a major source of marital strife? We think it is probably due to a few things: a failure to understand, or to live out, that there is no such thing as my money and your money, it's all God's money; a lack of unity in principles of managing money; and an inability to function through those stressful times of life in general. They're simple principles, but that does not make them easy to apply.

# ~ 9 ~

# On The Division of Labor

*Unless the Lord builds the house,*
*They labor in vain who build it;*
*Unless the Lord guards the city,*
*The watchman stays awake in vain.*

*It is vain for you to rise up early,*
*To sit up late,*
*To eat the bread of sorrows;*
*For so He gives His beloved sleep.*

— Psalm 127:1-2

## How Do You Figure Out Who Does What?

We weren't even married yet, and in fact were still in college, but Hal was already treading lightly on the subject. We grew up in traditional families with Dad going off to the plant or the office, Mom focusing on child rearing until both kids were in school, at which point she was free to teach school or find another daytime job.

But we had both grown up in public school and gone off to the university, where it was continually drummed into us that girls could and *ought to* do anything boys could do. You knew there was a political agenda behind that advice, but it influences you nevertheless.

So Hal broached the subject gingerly—did Melanie want to have a job outside the home, once they were married? After all, her studies in math and the sciences had been just as rigorous as Hal's in engineering, and at least in the beginning, before there were young children at home, the only consideration seemed to be whether or not Melanie wanted to enter the job market.

Melanie was quick to respond *NO*. Did Hal mean to push her in that direction? No, he didn't, but neither did he want to restrict her if that was her desire. He wanted his fiancée, and soon to be wife, to be as happy as he could make her.

As it happened, an outside career wasn't what she wanted at all. She didn't undervalue her academic training in the least, but her aspiration was not for Corporate America but for making a home for her husband and raising our children.

The awkward exchange illustrates the difficulty in even considering ideas which counter the prevailing culture. When society is pushing girls from their youngest age to aim for a career outside the home, a young woman whose heart is directed toward her family can feel isolated. The 20th Century brought a tremendous shift in the opportunities and the expectations for women. From the women's suffrage movement in the early 1900s to "Rosie the Riveter" in the 1940s and "Take Your Daughter to Work Day" now, the push has been for greater independence for women and an expectation that a woman will find her fulfillment in the workplace. In the job market, doors once closed to women were being flung open and invitations issued.[1] But let a young woman

---

[1] It has been interesting to note the evolution of corporate and academic recruiting materials we've received the past few decades. Brochures from Fortune 500 companies and major universities, concerned about a lack of cultural diversity in their past, have swung so far in the other

with math and science skills suggest that her calling lies at home, and she will quickly find herself on the "Traitors List" of her feminist sisters. Many girls who want to grow up and be a mother learn to say "an astronaut" or "a scientist" when adults ask what she wants to become—it's easier to explain, and people are more likely to smile and nod.

When we made that decision to buck the culture and live on a single, husband-provided income, we found friends which affirmed that choice. In our circle, "stay-at-home mother" is a title worn as proudly as "executive vice-president" in other places. Putting children in day care at an age when their world is still centered on Mother's arms seems far more unnatural than putting a career on hold to nurture them. Like our parents before us, we settled into a reasonably comfortable lifestyle: Hal worked for a corporation, Melanie cared for the children; Melanie cooked and managed the home, Hal cut grass and commuted. It worked for our parents, and it seemed to work pretty well for us—certainly better than the cycle of early day care-to-playschool-to-grade-school, Mom and Dad pursuing separate and sometimes conflicting careers, and lots of fast food and fish sticks along the way. We watched our neighbors' houses sitting quiet and empty most of the week, with the owners making overnight pit stops and weekend visits.

But then times changed. The economy went in the ditch. Fathers in mid-level management and professional staff like engineers and accountants were finding themselves on the far end of 99-week unemployment benefits. Many of our friends started small businesses to supplement or replace other income, with Mom working as hard as Dad to make ends meet. Sometimes Mom went to work and Dad stayed

---

direction that a young man looking at the brochure photographs might reasonably ask whether he starts at an automatic disadvantage now.

home, because her undergraduate degree was more in demand than his at the moment. Was that wrong, when a family found itself moved by circumstances in a direction they had tried hard to avoid?

When we answered Christ's call to be *in* the world but not *of* the world, we saw a balance to be struck. We needed to be aware of the culture around us, able to engage with it and challenge where it contradicted God's will, but remain unstained by it. There's more than one "world," though, in the sense that we could be out of God's will in either direction, toward an unbiblical freedom or an unbiblical restriction. So what does the Scripture say? Is the Biblical pattern for men to be the exclusive wage earners, and their wives to be exclusively devoted to domestic concerns? Are husband and wife free to exchange roles, so the wife becomes the breadwinner and the husband the bread maker? What is the balance?

## Biblical View of Division of Labor

The question of dividing up the work in a marriage is actually several questions—How should the family be supported? Are there tasks which are more appropriate for one spouse than the other? How should the household chores be divided?—for a start. Let's consider the high-level question—Who should provide the family's basic provision?

In creation, God ordained the man as the primary laborer, and the woman as his help. *The* LORD GOD PLANTED A GARDEN EASTWARD IN EDEN, AND THERE HE PUT THE MAN WHOM HE HAD FORMED. ...TO TEND AND TO KEEP IT.[2] The primary employment was assigned to the man, and then the Lord said, "It is *not good that man should be alone; I will make him a helper com-*

---

[2] Genesis 2:8, 15

*parable to him."*[3] The first woman was created to be a helper to her husband, the worker.

And that was the original design, before things went awry. When the first couple's distrust or disregard of God's direction led to sin, Adam's punishment was in his employment: *"Cursed is the ground for your sake,"* God said; *"In toil you shall eat of it All the days of your life ... In the sweat of your face you shall eat bread, Till you return to the ground..."*[4] On the other hand, Eve's curse didn't involve labor in the fields, but labor in childbearing—one thing unique to her, the one thing which Adam couldn't do.[5] It reaffirms that Eve's first role, to be a helper to her husband and to alleviate his loneliness—whether by her own presence or her ability to bring more people into the world—continues after the Fall.

The apostle Paul repeats this in his instructions to Titus, the church planting missionary on the island of Crete. He says that older men in the church are to be *"sober, reverent, temperate, sound in faith, in love, in patience,"* and older women, *"likewise."* Those women are told to *"admonish the young women to love their husbands, to love their children, to be discreet, chaste, homemakers, good, obedient to their own husbands..."*[6]

The premiere passage on the role of wives, of course, is Proverbs 31. Many reject its message, believing it to be a limitation on the true freedom of women; others embrace it with enthusiasm precisely because they think it supports women staying out of the workforce.

---

[3]  Genesis 2:18

[4]  Genesis 3:17, 19

[5]  Genesis 3:16

[6]  Titus 2:2-5

The interesting truth is somewhere in between. Yes, it definitely emphasizes the wife's role as a support and help to her husband, the tender of domestic cares:

> *The heart of her husband safely trusts her... She does him good and not evil, All the days of her life. ... She is like the merchant ships, She brings her food from afar. She also rises while it is yet night, And provides food for her household, And a portion for her maidservants. ... She is not afraid of snow for her household, for all her household is clothed in scarlet. She makes tapestry for herself; Her clothing is fine linen and purple. ...She looks well to the ways of her household and does not eat the bread of idleness.*[7]

But many people overlook, or never notice, the strong undercurrent of entrepreneurship. Yes, the Proverbs 31 woman is not just a homemaker—she's a businesswoman. Her husband *"will have no lack of gain,*[8] because she's not just feeding and clothing the family—she's got her eye on all sorts of opportunities:

> *She seeks wool and flax, And willingly works with her hands. ... She considers a field and buys it; From her profits she plants a vineyard. ... She perceives that her merchandise is good. And her lamp does not go out by night. She stretches out her hands to the distaff, And her hand holds the spindle. ... She makes linen garments and sells them, And supplies sashes to the merchant. ... Give her of the*

---

[7] Proverbs 31:11-12, 14-15, 21-22, 27
[8] Proverbs 31:11

*fruit of her hands, and let her own works praise
her in the gates.*[9]

While she is weaving and sewing to clothe her family, she
is also making textiles to sell directly or to provide to mer-
chants for resale. She gathers her profits and invests in real
estate, planting a vineyard which could be for family use or
possibly for commercial produce, as well. In fact, she works
long, productive hours to make the best use of her skills.
And the final verse says that she should receive "the fruit of
her own hands"—we would say she should get the benefit
of her productivity—and enjoy a public reputation for her
diligence and craftsmanship. It's to her husband's glory, but
she receives recognition on her own account, too.

In the tug-of-war over the role of women in the market-
place, this side of Proverbs 31 doesn't get enough discussion.
We might look at this sort of hand work and think of State
Fair competitions and church bazaars; we forget that when
Proverbs 31 was written, spinning and weaving were works of
provision, no less than plowing and harvesting. They weren't
just artisanal craftwork, they were serious labor. We do note,
however, that she is pursuing these in the context of her
home and family, not as an employee of someone else. That
definitely allows her to place a higher priority on the needs
of her husband and children.

This is a very difficult area to discuss. Melanie noticed years
ago that you could trace a change in our culture through the
newspaper's wedding announcements. When we got married,
typically the young groom had the same level of education
and same seriousness of job as his new wife—if not a little
more. Within the past ten or fifteen years, that's changed:
now it's rare to find a bride that's not better educated and

---

9 Proverbs 31:13, 16, 18-19, 24, 31

on a better career track than her new husband. Over years of counseling young mothers, Melanie has also noticed a growing lack of ambition and career focus among the young fathers. Unquestionably work is hard (a result of the Fall); if a young man has a wife willing to shift the burden of supporting the family off his shoulder, it's going to be a real temptation to let her, but this isn't the way it's supposed to work.

There are definitely situations where the husband *can't* provide, though it may be his wish. Paul told Timothy to *"Honor widows who are really widows,"* but cautioned him that it was the responsibility of the family first to take care of their own. *"But if any widow had children or grandchildren,"* he said, *"let them first learn to show piety at home and repay their parents; for this is good and acceptable before God."* [10] It's interesting that the widow is *not* commanded to go get a job, not even in the case of a younger widow, who is told to remarry to provide for her children. *"I desire that the younger widows marry, bear children, manage the house, give no opportunity to the adversary to speak reproachfully."*[11] Instead, adult children or grandchildren are expected to provide, giving us notice that we are responsible not just for our immediate family, but our extended family as well. If the family is unable to care for them, the church should.

What if neither the family nor the church is willing or able to help? Or if the husband is still living but incapacitated in some way, so his wife is not truly a widow? Then the wife needs to do what she can to take care of the family, but still in the context of being her husband's helper. In this case, the help he needs is in basic financial support for the home; it's still his area of concern, even if injury or illness has made it

---

[10] 1 Timothy 5:3-8
[11] 1 Timothy 5:14

impossible for him to work. If she's the breadwinner, biblically the wife is standing in for her husband.

For many years Hal worked as a full-time engineer for large corporations. As we changed our family's mission to pursue ministry and self-employment opportunities, Hal found part-time work as a subcontractor for an engineering firm. When the firm had more projects or bigger tasks than their staff employees could accomplish, they would call Hal in as temporary help. The project was still the firm's responsibility, and the client still held the firm accountable to complete the contract, but Hal was fulfilling a need for the firm.

When a wife finds herself in this position, she has to watch her heart and mind carefully toward her husband. The ability to provide the family's support is a powerful thing, and our enemy may use that occasion to try and disrupt the couple's relationship.

We have dear friends who set off to the mission field together, but a few years into the work the husband developed severe health issues which completely disabled him. The wife was able to continue in a different area of children's ministry to provide income for the family, and by the respect she and the children have publicly given their disabled father, it was blessedly plain that she continued to honor his leadership and position within the family.

Another family we know gradually lost their father to brain cancer. As he became more frail and less able to support or even to guide his family, the wife made sure that she and their children continue to treat him with deference, even while she was supporting the family in a prominent public role. We remember going out to dinner with them one night. The husband's mental acuity had faded to the point he was unable to communicate much at all, but throughout the evening she included him in our discussion, quietly explaining what was going on, speaking to him with gentleness, but as an adult and not a child. It was a tremendous, moving example of love, honor, and commitment in a marriage.

Sadly, there are homes, though, where the husband *won't* do what he is supposed to.

When Jesus spoke of God's provision for His people, He compared it to the support even a sinful man provides for his family: *"If you then, being evil, know how to give good gifts to your children, how much more will your Father who is heaven give good things to those who ask Him!"*[12]

If even the wicked know to provide for their children, then it should be obvious as a duty for the believer. Refusing to do so when one is capable may be more than simple laziness—it may signal a rejection of Christ. *[If] anyone does not provide for his own, and especially for those of his household,* warned Paul, he *has denied the faith and is worse than an unbeliever.*[13] The man who won't provide for his household should be held accountable and rebuked—by his wife, his church, his brothers in Christ.

## The Titus 2 Woman

When Paul wrote to Timothy concerning the relationships in his church, he said that older women in the congregation should be teaching the younger women to be *homemakers.*[14] Other translations have rendered it "keepers

---

[12] Matthew 7:11

[13] 1 Timothy 5:8

[14] Titus 2:3-4

at home", "working at home" or "workers at home", or "busy at home."

We've seen that particular term bent to fit the commentator's agenda, especially the rendering in the New International Version, where the older women are told to teach the younger wives "to be busy at home." One popular women's author took that verse and argued that it said almost nothing about outside employment for wives and mothers; rather, whenever a career-minded woman happened to find herself at home, well, she should make productive use of her time.

The term in the Greek is transliterated *oikourgos*. It only shows up that one time in the New Testament, but it's used in classical Greek as "the keeper of the house" or "one who keeps watch over the house." The part of the word translated "house" is also used in classical manuscripts to mean household or family. Melanie finds this really encouraging to think about: a wife and mother should be more than a housekeeper, as we would describe it, but should be a keeper of the household, like a lighthouse keeper who watches over the lighthouse, making sure the fires keep burning, or a garden-keeper who weeds and tends the garden, keeping out those pests that would despoil it. In the same way, we think this passage commands women to nurture their households, caring and tending for them.

Does this mean she can never engage in business outside the home? No, but we believe just as a faithful lighthouse keeper is always attending to the light even when he's hoeing his garden or writing in his diary, a mother's main priority has got to be her husband, children and home.

## So, how do these responsibilities look in reality?

It's a man's job to provide for his family. It's a woman's job to help her mate. That will look a little different in every family. In some families it will look just like we described at the start: Dad works a typical job away at an office or plant somewhere, and Mom does most of the housework (with the children's help, of course) since she is home more. There can be many variations on that arrangement, though.

Take for example, adding homeschooling into the picture. Home education is a full time job, especially if there are several children to teach. In most families, the daily task of home-schooling falls to Mom, and that means many of the things the mother might have done before will need to change—to be picked up by Dad or the children, or done more efficiently or less frequently, or maybe hired out.

Often re-assessing the work at home presents a fantastic opportunity to bless your children with regular chores.

Recently, Melanie was sitting at a Mother-Daughter Banquet across from a 17-year-old girl and her mother. After some conversation getting to know one another, the other mother asked what our other children were doing for dinner—had Melanie fixed them something or ordered them a pizza?

"I'm not sure *what* they're having," Melanie answered. "Whatever they decided to cook."

Both the mother and daughter were shocked. "Mom, I wouldn't know how to begin to fix a whole dinner!" exclaimed the daughter.

What a sad admission. This mom seemed like a very loving, concerned mother, but in her desire to make things as easy as possible for her children, she'd failed to teach her daughter a major life skill.

Chores are a good thing for children. They teach responsibility, diligence, and life skills. Bless your children by requiring them to contribute to the family mission.

## What about the rest of it, though?

We would suggest that the question of labor division in the marriage is less about who does what than it is about advancing the family mission, enjoying one another, and serving one another.

Any commander looks at his assets and decides how to deploy them based on what they can bring to the mission. Maybe Dad's a frustrated amateur chef who'd really, really rather own a restaurant? Then why shouldn't he be the family's primary cook? Is the wife a CPA who gave up accounting to stay home with the children? Then why would the big-picture husband who married her want to get mired in the details of family finances?

We've also discovered early in our marriage that we'd rather do things together so that we have company, than stick to the man's work/woman's work pattern our culture lays down. Neither of us are fond of yardwork or washing dishes, but we'd rather do both of them together than separately in "our" traditional roles. And there's nothing wrong with that!

Providing the main household income is the controversial question. When we were first married, we believed that Hal should earn all the money and Melanie should not have a outside job at all. It was our way of following Titus 2, letting Melanie be the "keeper at home."

As we studied Proverbs 31, we came to realize our ideas were perhaps more influenced by the culture of the 1950s than the Word of God. The exemplary wife in that chapter is very active in commerce and investment, all while maintaining her primary role at home in support of her husband's mission. She was free to buy and sell and interact with the business world within the context of being a wife and mother.

Because of this, we think it is perfectly all right for women to be a part of a family business, or to have a business of her own, with her husband's agreement . It's a huge challenge to keep everything in the right proportion, of course; we have to keep reminding ourselves that our marriage and our children are more important than our customers. For both men and women, that is the crux of the matter: What are your priorities?

A crucial matter which modern society has tried to down-play or ignore is the life-forming role of the mother-child relationship. It is different than the bond between father and child, and it's not something we can replace with a substitute.

God made women to be nurturers and managers of rela-tionships. Little girls are intensely interested in which child is best friends with whom, just like their mothers enjoying "chick flicks" on TV—no action is needed, if the interplay of characters and personalities is interesting.

Disruption to the very first relationship, between mother nd baby, can cause stress and even trauma to the child, with lifelong effects.[15] Even a short separation from his mother in the early hours after birth can have a yearlong effect on a child.[16] Repetitive separation, such as daycare, has a longer, more concerning effect which seems to increase with how long a young child has to endure separation.[17]

Our little ones, the weakest members of the household need to be the most protected and looked after members of the family, and yet because they can't clearly communicate and their personalities are still very self-focused, they often take the brunt of any emotional upheaval in our lives.

One of our friends worked in an office full of women. She said that young expectant mothers just assumed they'd put the children in daycare and everything would be fine; after all, that's what they'd been told for years, and that's just the way it's done, right?

When the babies came, though, everything changed. Time and again our friend watched the traumatic return from maternity leave, as the broken-hearted new mothers talked tearfully about their babies, frequently calling the daycare or the sitter to check on them. Over the weeks, though, their

[15] Graham, YP, C. Heim, et al. "The Effects of Neonatal Stress on Brain Development: Implications for Psychopathology." *National Center for Biotechnology Information.* U.S. National Library of Medicine, Summer 1999. Web. 29 Aug. 2012. <http://www.ncbi.nlm.nih.gov/pubmed/10532624>.

[16] Bystrova, K., V. Ivanova, et al. "Early Contact versus Separation: Effects on Mother-infant Interaction One Year Later." *National Center for Biotechnology Information.* U.S. National Library of Medicine, June 2009. Web. 29 Aug. 2012. <http://www.ncbi.nlm.nih.gov/pubmed/19489802>.

[17] Belsky, Ph.D., Jay, Institute for the Study of Children, Families and Social Issues, Birkbeck University of London, UK. "Early Day Care and Infant-Mother Attachment Security." *Encyclopedia on Early Childhood Development.* Center of Excellence for Early Childhood Development, Oct. 2009. Web. 29 Aug. 2012. <http://www.child-encyclopedia.com/documents/belskyangxp-attachment.pdf>.

hearts would gradually grow cold, the calls and tears would fade away, until they hardly ever mentioned their little ones at work and it seemed not a big deal at all.

If you have no choice, you trust that God will take care of the situation, but God made mothers and babies to be together and growing accustomed to being apart doesn't change that. Can't we say to these new mothers, "The way you feel is normal! You're not supposed to be apart. Go home!"

## Bringing the Family On Board

If it is at all possible, separation of mothers and young children, really *any* children, should be avoided as much as possible. We've tried to steer a course for more inclusion of the young children with our "grown up" activities whenever possible. When Hal took business trips, often he arranged to bring Melanie and the children along. When we began speaking to parent groups and convention audiences, we took the kids—all the way down to nursing babes—on the trip. In fact, Melanie has made it a point to always bring our children less than two with us, no matter what. The longest Melanie's comfortable leaving a little one with someone else is about long enough to give an hour-long workshop. Occasionally, in a pinch, we've even spoken with a wakeful infant in our arms! (Obviously, this is more plausible at a family-life retreat than a technical conference).

It takes some creativity and compromise to pull this off, but we do our best to bring all of the children still home with us—and sometimes even our adult children take off and join us. We drive rather than fly, in most cases, and sometimes we camp or stay in people's homes along the way to avoid paying for two hotel rooms (remember, we have a lot of kids). We make sandwiches or eat in family-friendly places instead of upscale, expense-account restaurants. The sacrifices and trade-offs have been worth it, though; we've decided we didn't want to lose our children in the process of advising other parents on raising theirs. This kind of inclusion, if you're able to make it happen, can build family unity and reduce the children's resentment when business takes up your time and attention. It's amazing how observant the children are, too, and the new perspective they can bring to your business.

These possibilities are one reason for a growing interest in entrepreneurial business among Christians. It is easiest to keep the right priorities for your work-life balance if you or your mate owns the business, even though you will probably work way more hours for yourself than you had to work for your last employer.

That's way easier than when either of you, but a wife in particular, works for someone else. When a wife works for someone outside the home, especially if she's an employee rather than an independent contractor, she may find her loyalties and priorities mixed or torn. It places her between two earthly masters, both of whom want the best of her time and energy. Making the turmoil worse, often outside jobs provide more immediate and measurable payoffs (both in praise and paychecks) than the work waiting at home. Babies don't generally thank you for changing their diapers and nine-year-olds practically never thank you for disciplining them. This can tempt a mom to spend even more time and effort outside the home, where the rewards are more tangible.

The same things can happen with volunteer work; we've seen it where a volunteer in one ministry or another ends up distracted from their family responsibilities because the need of the charity seems so great and the thanks of the organization or their beneficiaries are so vocal. It happens to men as well as women.

Should you avoid volunteer or ministry work? Certainly not, but neither should your service to the church or community become a source of resentment and suffering for your family. Whether it's unpaid service or profitable business, we can't allow ourselves to be diverted from our primary focus and mission. For mothers, it's the care and nurture of the family God has given them to serve.

## It's a Balance

Like many things in the Christian life, the division of work in a marriage and a family is a matter of balance. Fathers need to work hard to support their families and not allow their wives to take on more of the burden than they can handle. Husbands need to embrace their responsibility. And wives need to see to their own households before they consider other opportunities, remembering that their little ones need *them* way more than they need a nicer car or trendy clothes. From time to time throughout our lives, that balancing point may be in different arrangements; that's okay. Let's just keep our priorities straight.

*So God created man in His own image;*
**in the image of God He created him;**
*male and female He created them.*

— Genesis 1:27

## ~ 10 ~

# The Spiritual Aspect

*But as for me and my house, we will serve the Lord.*
— Joshua 24:15 ESV

A t a conference recently we spoke with a woman who had questions about dealing with her rebellious teenaged son. As she shared her situation, she painted a picture of change and stress in their family—the death of a parent, the new widow moving into their home, the challenges and transitions of early adolescence, and an ongoing context of religious and cultural differences between the husband and wife. There was obviously love between them, but not a unified purpose toward their family life.

Hal encouraged her to be constant in her faithfulness to God and her respect and loyalty to her husband, even though he didn't share her commitment to Christ. He also pointed out that because marriage was a universal, God-ordained institution which didn't rest on a particular religious tradition, it was right for her to look to her husband for support, protection, and guidance, regardless of his personal philosophy or belief system.

The apostles Peter and Paul both spoke of the Christian in a mixed-faith marriage.[1] Although a follower of Jesus should not marry outside the faith, it is not uncommon, for one reason or another, for a believer to find him- or herself wed-

---

[1] 1 Peter 3:1, 1 Corinthians 7:12-16

ded to a non-believer. This is a particular challenge for the believing spouse.

Yet Paul makes it very clear that our marriage is designed to give the world an illustration of God's love, as two individuals are knit together into one, and God gives them grace to love, forgive, bear with, and bear up one another. There are incredible things going on beyond the visible world as God works through our union, because it is a union of whole persons—body, mind, and spirit. It is more than a legalized living arrangement, it is a profoundly spiritual *process*. To become all it should be, your marriage must be working for a spiritual unity as well as a comfortable agreement between friends.

## True Christianity

Many religions make much of obedience, observance, and ritual. The religion of Christianity is also a matter of relationship. When God created the first human beings, He did not send messengers and signs to communicate with them; He came down to them and walked among them Himself. When they were unfaithful to Him, He did not simply destroy the earth and start over, but provided One who would take their place before God's seat of judgment—in fact, an innocent One who would suffer the death sentence God pronounced on such treason.

That One, Jesus Christ, was sent by God the Father because God *loved the world*.[2] What's more, when the Son of God came to walk among men just as God His Father had done, He did not simply appear to them as a visible spirit. He did not cover Himself with human form like a mechanic puts on overalls before tackling the dirty job ahead. Instead, Christ *became*

---

[2] John 3:16

*flesh*. He took our nature as His own. Being fully divine, He added full humanity to His nature.

God calls us to obedience, but He calls us to *love* Him and to love His Son Jesus. It's a relationship, and just like our relationship with our mate, it takes time, humility, communication, and thought to build it up. If we want to strengthen the spiritual side of our marriage, we need to start with our individual spiritual health.

## It's important to keep up devotional life

The first step of course is establishing our relationship to God and Christ. Have we honestly come to grips with our guilt—not the *feeling*, but the *fact*, that we have broken God's commandments and failed to live up to His standard, and richly deserve God's anger and final judgment? When God created man and woman and the institution of marriage, He gave them simple instructions to obey. When the first couple chose to ignore God's warnings and put their own curiosity and desires ahead of the Creator's commandment, they plunged themselves, their descendents, and indeed, all of Creation, into a valley of brokenness, decay, and death. Sin does that.

God tells us plainly that *"There is none righteous, no, not one;... all have sinned and fall short of the glory of God."*[3] Our best efforts to clean up our act will fail, because God's purity is so high above ours that *we are all like an unclean* thing, *and all our righteousnesses are like filthy rags* in His sight.[4]

So if we're already condemned by our past actions, and God says we can't work our way back into His favor, our only hope

[3] Romans 3:10, 23
[4] Isaiah 64:6

is the mercy of the court, so to speak. Only if we've come to Him in humility and asked for His forgiveness, acknowledging our fault and our helplessness in the face of our guilt, can we expect any positive reward at the end of this life. The Puritans used to speak of King Jesus, to remind themselves that He is not only the King above all earthly kings, but our refusal to submit to His rule is an act of spiritual rebellion. We have to give up our lives of insurrection against God's ways, turn ourselves over to Him, and come into His camp. *"I am the way, the truth, and the life,"* Jesus told His disciples. *"No man comes to the Father except through Me."*[5]

When we've joined the ranks of His disciples, we have to nurture the relationship. Jesus said, *"If anyone loves Me, he will keep My word; and My Father will love him, and We will come to him and make Our home with him."*[6] We need to know His word in order to keep it, so we should to make it our goal to be familiar with the Bible and refresh our understanding regularly. We need to remember Him as we go through our days, take time to talk with Him in prayer, and give Him honor and thanks for every thing He sends into our lives—both the pleasant and the unpleasant, remembering that *God works all things together for good to those who love God and are called according to His purpose.*[7]

Most believers will acknowledge this is a disciplined life which is challenging to maintain. We are generally busy, easily distracted, often tired, and frankly lazy. Yet without making the effort, we risk hearts which grow cold and distant toward the One who died in our place and now claims our love and obedience. That in turn will make our love toward our mate and family more fragile as well. Yet it's all too easy

---

[5] John 14:6
[6] John 14:23
[7] Romans 8:28

to let it slip one day, and the next, and before long, you can't remember the last time you drew near to God outside of a church service.

So what can we do to carve out time for personal devotion?

Melanie struggled with this when our children were small. In the hectic life of a young mother, she could never remember to read her Bible at time when it was actually possible. One day, overwhelmed with frustration, she asked the Lord to help her find time to spend with Him. She remembers praying, "Lord, if You will just remind me to have devotions at a time I can do it, I won't say no to You." Has she ever failed on that promise? Yes, she admits that it's happened repeatedly, yet she's found the Lord reminds her every day as soon as she wakes up. To make it simple, she finally put a Bible in the bathroom!

Hal has used different approaches throughout our marriage. The most useful is when he's had a regular schedule and could get up early each morning for time in the Word before leaving for work. When the schedule has been cramped or irregular, or morning times too busy for the rest of the family, he's taken a small Bible in his briefcase or lunchbox, reading during a break or at lunchtime. He's loaded electronic versions on his PDA or smart phone, and listened to Bible recordings while commuting or traveling—an excellent way to redeem oft-wasted time on the road.

*You will seek me and find me, when you seek me with all your heart.*[8]

It's a wonderful truth that God knows our weakness and failure, and loves us in spite of them. When we realize we've wandered away from Him, He welcomes us back just as the father of the Prodigal Son did—with joy, forgiveness, and love. If you realize you need to be spending more time with Him, just ask for forgiveness and start again!

## How does the Gospel affect your marriage?

In the book of Ecclesiastes, the Preacher observes that

> *Two are better than one, because they have a good reward for their toil. For if they fall, one will lift up his fellow. But woe to him who is alone when he falls and has not another to lift him up! Again, if two lie together, they keep warm, but how can one keep warm alone? And though a man might prevail against one who is alone, two will withstand him—a threefold cord is not quickly broken.*[9]

When both husband and wife are Christians, there are particular blessings in marriage. You can pray for one another, encourage one another in the Lord, even rebuke one another in love when necessary. When there is conflict or stress between you, the Holy Spirit is there to convict us where we've sinned and empower us to reconcile with one another. The threefold cord the Preacher describes is the two of you plus the Lord and that bond is not easily broken. Serving the Lord together gives your marriage more strength and more

---

[8] Jeremiah 29:13 ESV
[9] Ecclesiastes 4:9-12 ESV

joy, and if one of you is a new believer, there is rejoicing in heaven as well as in your home.

## What if one spouse is not a believer?

In the years of explosive missionary expansion of the gospel, the church was full of new converts, mostly adults, and doubtless many came into the faith before their spouses. The same thing happens today. What did the apostles say about the situation?

Writing to the Corinthians, the apostle Paul advised, *"If any brother has a wife who does not believe, and she is willing to live with him, let him not divorce her. And a woman who has a husband who does not believe, if he is willing to live with her, let her not divorce him."*[10]

Peter wrote to the churches in his care that the loving example of a believing wife, freely submitted to her husband in spite of their spiritual disagreement, could be the means of bringing him to examine the gospel for himself. *"Wives... be submissive to your own husbands, that even if some do not obey the word, they, without a word, may be won by the conduct of their wives, when they observe your chaste conduct* accompanied *by fear."*[11]

Paul warned there was no guarantee—*"For how do you know, O wife, whether you will save your husband? Or how do you know, O husband, whether you will save your wife?"*[12]—but the hope is there. In some situations, simply living for Christ will speak more loudly than words do; as Paul said, we be-

---

[10] 1 Corinthians 7:12-13
[11] 1 Peter 3:1-2
[12] 1 Corinthians 7:16

come *"living epistles"* [13] that demonstrate the power of Christ in our daily walk.

## Family Worship

The apostle John, in his third letter, wrote, *"I have no greater joy than to hear that my children walk in truth."* [14] The patriarch Abraham received a special revelation from God because he would faithfully teach his children *"and they shall keep the way of the LORD ..."* [15] Paul instructed fathers to *"bring [your children] up in the nurture and admonition of the Lord."* [16]

It is a blessed duty of Christian parents to teach their kids to know and love the Lord God. When God established the nation of Israel, Moses laid out a pattern of constant instruction:

> *And these words that I command you today shall be on your heart. You shall teach them diligently to your children, and shall talk of them when you sit in your house, and when you walk by the way, and when you lie down, and when you rise.* [17]

This is probably one of the most neglected things among serious Christians. We seem to think our children will just pick up what we believe because they live in our homes and we take them to church (and after all, that's why we pay to hire youth pastors, right?) Yet time and again, we are amazed by the number of people our age, mostly professing Christians themselves, who aren't sure whether their parents are

[13] 2 Corinthians 3:2. Much of the New Testament was originally written as letters (epistles) to individuals or churches.

[14] 3 John 1:4 (KJV)

[15] Genesis 18:17-19 (KJV)

[16] Ephesians 6:4 (KJV)

[17] Deuteronomy 6:6-7

believers or not. "They always took me to church, but they never talked about God, really," they say.

That's sad. It's also a tragic omission, if the parents are Christians.

One effective way to pass our faith along to our children is to hold regular devotions as a family. It was once expected that Christian fathers would lead the family in daily prayers and Bible reading, as a minimum; usually anyone in the household, from honored guests to servants and apprentices, would be included. This is what Abraham was doing, when the Lord said, "*I have chosen him, that he may command his children and his household after him to keep the way of the LORD...*"[18]

This can be done any number of ways. We find it's more helpful to be regular with a short time of teaching and worship, than to plan elaborate and lengthy devotions which we can't maintain from day to day. The simplest way is to choose a book of the Bible and read through it, no more than a chapter a day, and often somewhat less (it depends on the book you've chosen, and the age and maturity of the family members). As you read, explain the passage and try to answer any questions. Sing a hymn together (we like to sing the same hymn each day for a week, to teach all the verses). Close with prayer for the family's concerns. We try to keep it short but consistent.

Some will object that they don't have training or even an idea how to start explaining a passage. A good devotional guide can help develop your teaching skills. Charles Spurgeon's *Morning and Evening* is a time-proven example. Matthew Henry's commentary is well-respected and practically devotional rather than academic in style.

---

[18] Genesis 18:19 (ESV)

A less-familiar resource we found tremendously helpful is J.C. Ryle's *Expository Thoughts on the Gospels*. A friend gave us this four-volume set as a wedding present, and we used it for our family devotions when there were just two of us. Ryle, an evangelical Anglican bishop from the end of the 19th century, starts with the book of Matthew and breaks it into manageable daily readings, with only a couple of pages of commentary on each selection. It's conversational in style and focuses on the basic point of the passage rather than complex interpretations. By the time we worked through to the gospel of John, Ryle was making longer comments, but we had learned how to read a passage and look for the key lessons.

## Encouraging the children to take part

Sooner than we think, our children will be adults themselves, and it's important that we train them to be comfortable thinking and talking about the Lord publicly. We encourage our children to participate in devotions by asking questions, sharing prayer requests, and praying aloud themselves when we have time. Our older children are asked to share insights and applications from the passage. They will soon be leading their own families and need to be able to teach.

## Singing

What about singing? It's an important part of both instruction and worship. Paul wrote to the Colossian church, *"Let the word of Christ dwell in you richly in all wisdom; teaching and admonishing one another in psalms and hymns and spiritual songs, singing with grace in your hearts to the Lord."*[19] Our songs are not just expressions of love and praise to Jesus, but also

---

[19] Colossians 3:16 KJV

express truth, rebuke sin, and encourage faithful obedience to God's commands.

If you are uncertain about singing together—don't be! It's an unusual young child who doesn't love singing, and your children really don't care whether you can stay on key or not. If you don't have a hymnbook, you can often find them in used bookstores; we got a boxful from a church which was replacing theirs. If you need help with tunes, get a CD or find a website which has recordings of hymns—there are several. .

## Who Should Take The Lead?

In the grand scheme of job allocation, is this the responsibility of the husband or the wife? The father, or the mother?

The pattern in Scripture is consistently pointing to the father as the spiritual head of the family. We have the example of Abraham; the ringing challenge of Joshua, *"As for me and my house, we will serve the Lord"*[20]; and the apostles' admonitions for fathers to teach their children (not to mention Paul's expectation that wives look to their husbands for spiritual guidance).[21] There is also the counter example of Eli, whose sons' irreverent behavior as priests let God to declare, *"I am about to punish his house forever, for the iniquity that he knew, because his sons were blaspheming God, and he did not restrain them."*[22] Granted, Eli, as high priest, had a double responsibility to restrain his sons who were serving under him, but it's still a serious warning.

Yet even though the father bears the primary responsibility, mothers should be teaching their children, as well. *My son,*

[20] Joshua 1;9
[21] 1 Corinthians 14:35
[22] 1 Samuel 3:13 ESV

*hear the instruction of your father, And do not forsake the law of your mother,* says the proverb.[23] A mother usually spends the most time with her children and she should take advantage of that to teach them the things of God. Both parents should be disciples themselves, and striving to make disciples of their children.

If the husband is not exercising spiritual headship in the home, and isn't teaching the children as he should, the Scripture certainly allows the wife to teach the children herself. Paul's young missionary colleague Timothy was the son of a Greek father and a believing Jewish mother, and Paul associates Timothy's faith with that of his mother and also-believing grandmother.[24] If a wife finds herself in this position, she needs to be careful to maintain her respect toward him; it is not helpful to announce, "Children, since your father won't teach you, let's have devotions." Instead, she should continue to privately appeal to him to lead the family in devotions, and until he does, choose a time for devotions when Dad is busy elsewhere—not to be secretive, but to avoid drawing the children's attention to his omission.

Many times fathers are just tired or forgetful, so if he has said that he wants the family to have devotions, it may be helpful to ask, "Honey, what I can I do to help you? Do you want me to gather the children at a certain time, or would you like for me to discreetly remind you?"

Family worship may seem like a burden or feel awkward at first, but it is an investment in your children's souls. So is taking the family to church.

---

[23] Two proverbs, actually—Proverbs 1:8 and 6:20
[24] Acts 16:1, 2 Timothy 1:5

## Church

God deals with each of His children as individuals; we can't be saved on the merits of anyone but Christ, and neither our parents or our association with one group or another will secure God's mercy toward us. It is interesting to note, though, that from the very start He placed His new believers in the family of a local assembly. It's where we find fellowship, encouragement, teaching, and accountability as believers. God has placed a particular blessing on the gathering of believers and calls teachers and leaders to guide them in His ways.

It's our responsibility to place ourselves in a local church gathering. The writer to the Hebrews said, *And let us consider how to stir up one another to love and good works, not neglecting to meet together, as is the habit of some, but encouraging one another, and all the more as you see the Day [of Christ's return] drawing near.*[25]

Once it was rare to meet a Christian family that did not have a church home. Now we meet them all the time. Some families have just fallen out of the habit. Some say that they don't need "church" to worship God—which is true as far as it goes; Biblically speaking, we should be thinking of God and His ways all the time, whether alone or in the company of other believers, but that doesn't give us permission to simply ignore His direction to gather together. Others say they've been hurt by churches that abused their authority. It happens—we've known several families in this situation, in different places. Again, finding yourself injured by a local church which is misguided (or misled) doesn't give you permission to abandon the fellowship of all other churches, too.

---

[25] Hebrews 10:24-25

One trend we find alarming are those that say that they "home church." They don't mean they meet with other Christian families in a home rather than a church building—that is perfectly Biblical—but instead, they simply gather their household around them for devotions on Sunday and call that "church."

Is there ever a place for that? Certainly. You may experience what our old church used to call "providential hinderances," events or circumstances beyond your control that keep you from meeting in your regular fellowship; a road-closing snowstorm comes to mind. Sometimes we may stay home from a worship service to avoid sharing a nasty virus with our friends at church. Sometimes we've been traveling in places or on schedules that make it difficult, impossible, or even dangerous to meet with local believers. Spending a longer-than-usual time for family devotions on Sunday may be our best observance of the Lord's Day.

But in the midst of many reasons or excuses for not joining together with other families of believers on a regular basis, we have to be honest with ourselves before God—are we *neglecting to meet together, as is the habit of some?*

Please know that we understand how hard it can be. We too have been under pastors who overstepped their authority and hurt families. We've traveled on business and ministry for weeks on end and struggled to be able to attend anywhere. We've had weeks of sickness that kept us away from church. But it is critically important that you have teaching, accountability, and fellowship from others. It helps protect us from our own error and sin. We need people who are built into our lives (and us, built into theirs) to rebuke us and lift us up as we need. The fellowship of like-minded Christians can be a river of blessings; we've leaned on the support and love of our church fellows through cancer treatment, children in ICU, and other crises. We are truly family to one another.

## Finding a Church

When we happen to mention our church to someone, often they say, "I wish my church was like that, but it's not." Let's talk first about finding a good church if you are without one, and then about knowing when to change churches.

## Are they teaching the Gospel?

The book of Acts describes the assemblies of the early church, where the Christians devoted themselves to fellowship, the breaking of bread (generally meaning the sacrament of the Lord's Supper), the apostles' teaching, and prayer.

The very first criterion we look for in a church is the teaching. Are they sharing the Gospel and the basic essentials of the faith? Do they teach that Jesus Christ is fully God and fully man, led a sinless life, died on the cross as a payment for our sins, and rose again from the dead? Do they teach salvation is by grace alone through faith alone? If not, you and your children will not hear the words of life there.

We also look for a church which is true to the Scriptures—not a particular translation, but the original Hebrew and Greek. Do they teach that the Bible in its original language is the inerrant and infallible Word of God? If a church has rejected the Bible as the only reliable and binding rule of faith and practice, then their teaching will be commandments and opinions of men. Once the you find church built on the foundation of Christ and the apostles, teaching the truth about Jesus, salvation, and God's word, then you can begin to look at other things.

If the church meets the standard on the essentials, how close is it to your own theological positions? *O, how good and pleasant it is for brethren to dwell together in unity,* says the Psalmist, and we do find a particular comfort when we don't have a continual doctrine check running when we gather for worship.[26] We never want to lose the Berean spirit (the book of Acts describes the believers in Berea as "more noble" than others, because they heard the apostles' teaching and always compared it to Scripture), but there is a freedom in our worship and study when we are in agreement on a wide range of Biblical issues. It's especially helpful when you have children to be in a church fellowship where you don't have to continually explain, "Well, that's not exactly what we believe..."

We know from experience, though, that sometimes you have to take what you can get! We've lived in cities that literally had only three churches which held to the Gospel and the Scriptures, and none of them quite suited our theological bent. Did we stop going to church? Certainly not. We thanked God we had believers of *any* denomination to meet with and chose the church closest to what we preferred.

Sometimes God will use these times we have to "settle" for a different denomination or style of church. Through our time in military and several job relocations, we have associated ourselves with churches in at least seven different denominations, from Baptist to Brethren, Presbyterian to Fundamentalist, and Alliance to non-denominational churches. Each one has blessed us in some way, and we've had our faith strengthened in unexpected area. The crucial thing we've learned is that God's people are not concentrated in a single

---

[26] Psalm 133:1

denomination, and we can find fellowship in many different congregations.

## What If You And Your Spouse Come From Different Traditions?

Maybe the two of you come from different church backgrounds within Christianity. How do you address that?

When we first started to realize there was potential for more than just friendship between us, we had some denominational differences to sort out. Hal came from a historically Methodist family but grew up in a moderate Presbyterian church. When he was saved in college, he moved to a more conservative group among the Presbyterian denominations. Melanie, on the other hand, was saved as a child and had grown up Baptist, being involved with Southern Baptist, Free Will, and Independent Baptist churches over the years.[27]

About the time we started courting, Hal finished a careful study of the issue of baptism and found himself more in agreement with Baptist teaching on that ordinance. That helped. However, there was a serious potential conflict in the way the two of us approached evangelism and the Gospel. We agreed that we both knew it and believed it, but how should it be preached? How should it be shared with the world? Do Presbyterian Calvinists *really* believe the good news should be taught to everybody? Do Independent Baptists *really* believe that God is sovereign over how individuals respond to the

---

[27] You may not know it from the outside, but both the Presbyterian and Baptist worlds host a wide range of denominations and practices. There are organizations in both camps which hold to stricter or looser views of the Bible, broader or narrower presentations of the Gospel, more or less social justice in their service projects and greater or lesser passion for missions.

gospel? *What do you mean by that interpretation? And where would we ever go to church?*

## Different approaches to the problem

There are several ways to approach a conflict of this sort. You could decide it's a deal breaker and end the courtship. You could agree to disagree and seek out separate places of worship. You might decide the particular difference is not that important, and one of you relinquish your position in favor of the other. You could call a truce and go someplace with a different tradition altogether.

We chose to work through the issues and try to come to a point of mutual understanding, since we were both believers and by that time in our lives, our differences had grown much less. It made for a very good time of Bible study together, a lot of edifying conversation, and some interesting reading swapped back and forth. Eventually we both learned more than we thought we knew at the start. Moving several times across the country in our early marriage gave us opportunities to unite with different churches, often finding our choices limited, as we mentioned, by simple availability. We came eventually to being in complete agreement.

As he wrapped up his time of leadership in Israel, Moses told them that *"The secret things belong to the LORD our God, but those things which are revealed belong to us and to our children forever, that we may do all the words of this law."*[28] We need to remember that there are doctrinal issues which God has not fully opened to us, and while theologians may have worked out consistent but differing interpretations, some of those differences will never be resolved this side of heaven. While we both agree on the purpose and method of baptism,

[28] Deuteronomy 29:29

it's been debated by deeply godly men for centuries. The style of music in worship is often a matter of taste rather than doctrine, as is much of the style of preaching. Our time in different churches has taught us to hold to what we believe with grace toward other viewpoints, We are committed to teaching our children the whole Bible, not just the convenient parts, and part of that means recognizing where God has left room for liberty and personal convictions, too.

So, among the churches which are teaching the Gospel and hold to a strong view of Scripture, we suggest you choose one that is as compatible as you can find within your own theological convictions—but don't rule out other possibilities, too.

## Other Aspects of the Life of the Church

Unfortunately, there are many churches whose documents say the right things, but the church doesn't reflect it. Sometimes you find pastors and elders preaching truth to a resisting congregation. We've been in some. Listen in to what people are talking about. Do they discuss the teaching? Do they sound like real believers? Do they show a serious concern about the things of God? The life of the church should be one of growth in maturity, as a normal thing.

We like to see a church with children present in the worship service with their parents; we helped change the culture of one congregation when we routinely kept our kids with us instead of sending them to the nursery.[29]

---

[29] It can be done, if taught consistently from a young age and carried out with patience and sensitivity on the part of the parents. We were able to train our young children to sit quietly through a worship service, though we had to be ready to take them out if they became restless or distracting to the congregation.

## No church is perfect

All that said, no church is going to be perfect. You look for the best compromise you can without giving up the essentials of the faith. You may find that you need to drive; we've attended churches less than five minutes from our home, and others an hour drive or more. Closer is better because it facilitates building into each other's lives and is so much easier to make it to meetings during the week, but sometimes the more distant church is a much better a fit. Some churches who have many members coming from far away have a covered dish meal every Sunday. This makes Sunday less of a burden for for traveling families, and it allows families from both near and far to know each other better.

## Should You Change Churches?

It's hard to say when you should stay in a church and when you should go. If the pastor or elders are not teaching the essentials of the faith, it's time to go, but what about if the church is just not satisfying you in less critical ways? Perhaps the teaching is weak and not meaty enough. Maybe most of the families are not really engaged in the church. Maybe you find your family life and convictions changing from the rest and you are feeling lonely. The demographics of the church may have changed and your family isn't finding as much fellowship.

Generally, the best answer is to stay and serve God. Don't be quick to leave a church without making sure first that the Lord hasn't put you there to influence it. We've moved a lot in our marriage, literally from coast to coast, so we have a lot of experience in different churches. We remember attending one church where we were the only ones to bring our children into the service with us. We were extra careful to make sure they were not at all disruptive and people began commenting positively on their behavior. By the time we left the church, years later, nearly everyone had their children in corporate worship with them.

You may also need to stay in an uncomfortable church situation *because your own sins are being addressed*. It might be an awkward sermon series on an embarrassing topic, a seriously damaged relationship with another member, or a direct case of church discipline which puts us on the hot seat. Sometimes it's exactly what we need for our spiritual health. We have been in churches where a father was (quite rightfully) confronted by the elders over a serious ongoing sin, and while it would have been easy for him and his family to simply depart and start over in another church, they chose to submit to their church leaders, repent of the sin, and work for reconciliation all around. And they had the love and support of the entire church as they went through the process.

## When You May Need To Leave

On the other hand, sometimes you may realize that an issue in question is too important to ignore, or you don't have the influence you need to serve God effectively there, or that your own family is suffering in some way that could be improved by changing churches. It's something that shouldn't be lightly done, and should be done in as peaceful and non-dissentious way as possible. When it's necessary to leave, though, sometimes it is a great relief to get into a church that is more likeminded and consistently serious about the Christian life.

There are other times that will require that you leave and leave quickly. If it becomes plain that a church leader is a wolf in sheep's clothing, the best course is to flee. False teaching, denial of fundamental doctrines, open sin among the leadership or abuse of their office in an attempt unbiblically control families are all signs to find another church home.

## Trying To Flourish Where You're Planted

When you find the perfect church, you'll see it's made up of perfect people. That won't happen until we all reach heaven. Anything on earth will require a compromise between the ideal and the attainable. In the process of resolving our disagreements and learning to live in grace with other redeemed sinners, as we give and receive God's love through the gathered family of faith, as we receive God's word through the faithful teaching of His word, we will be growing in faith and love, and proclaiming God's goodness and righteousness to our community, our children, and to one another.

# ~ 11 ~

# Being of One Mind

*Therefore if there is any consolation in Christ, is any comfort of love, any participation in the Spirit, any affection and sympathy, complete my joy by being of the same mind, having the same love, being in full accord and of one mind.*

— Philippians 2:1-2

In his later years, when Martin Luther was in a jovial mood, he referred to his wife Katherine as "my rib." Our second daughter is named after Katherine Luther. She is the only child Hal calls by a nickname; Luther's wife was commonly called Katie. In modern times, an affectionate husband might sometimes call his spouse "my other half" or "my *better* half." Given their natural bias toward individualism and independence, it's probably good for men to remind themselves of their dependence on their wives. Likewise, given the rise of feminism and the increasing emphasis that young women develop their own careers and an independent spirit, such a reminder may be more needful for women than it once was. The two have become one flesh, and we are both part of a greater unity—our marriage.

We had a reminder of this dependency recently when Hal underwent chemotherapy for lymphoma. He was spared many of the worst side effects, but one which surprised us was a definite change in his level of attention and memory.

Melanie was startled when he began forgetting tasks and appointments which he normally juggled adroitly. When she pointed this out, we both realized we'd have to keep a check on each other to make sure everything was being done according to schedule and expectation. For a time, Hal thought of Melanie as one half of his brain.

This could have been even more difficult than it was. Thankfully, Hal had learned to give and expect a second opinion about important actions while he was working for the power company. In that business, working around transmission lines and substation switchgear, a slip of concentration or a moment of distraction could black out large parts of a city—or kill a co-worker. The utility company trained its workers to look over each other's shoulder, literally, and to carefully consider what they were about to do before taking action. Not everyone is willing to take advice, but it served us well when we had to keep our family and business on the move while Hal was undergoing medical treatment.

However, it wasn't just the utility experience that made things work for our family. It was really rooted in years of trust and confidence toward one another beforehand. Because he was secure in her respect and loyalty, Hal could admit to Melanie, "Hey, I'm having trouble keeping track of things—can you help me?" And that security didn't "just happen."

## What the Bible Says About Unity [or Trust]

One of the earliest statements about marriage describes the union of husband and wife: *Therefore a man shall leave his father and his mother and be joined to his wife, and they shall become one flesh.*[1] This is one of the fundamental

---

[1] Genesis 2:24

truths about marriage—it takes two individuals and makes them into a new, unified entity. He and She become We.

Other passages illustrate the broad ramifications of this truth. *This is a great mystery,* Paul writes to the Ephesians.[2] There is a sexual aspect to it, demonstrated when Paul warns against the hidden implications of casual intimacy: *Or do you not know that he who is joined to a harlot is one body* with her? *For "the two", He says,"shall become one flesh."* [3] We discuss this in greater detail elsewhere, but there is a spiritual union which is as real and permanent as a corporeal, physical connection. Jesus quotes the verse from Genesis to teach against divorce,[4] and Paul argues that a husband's love for his wife and his willingness to sacrifice himself on her behalf is no less than a man's care for his own health and comfort.[5]

In fact, Paul completes the circle with the church in Corinth, when he says, *The wife does not have authority over her own body, but the husband* does. *And likewise the husband does not have authority over his own body, but the wife* does.[6] He is writing about the sexual union of a husband and wife, but he words the principle more broadly. Within the union of marriage, there is a commingling of persons deeply enough that each loses autonomy over their own physical being.

Obviously, apart from the short moments of physical intimacy, the husband and wife still exist in two bodies. They don't grow together like trees intertwined as saplings. There are still two brains and two hearts. The continuing union takes place in the non-material side of things, the realm of the mind, emotions, spirit and soul. As profound as sexual

2 Ephesians 5:32
3 1 Corinthians 6:16
4 Matthew 19:3-6 and Mark 6:6-9
5 Ephesians 5: 28-31
6 1 Corinthians 7:4

union is, there is much about it that comes naturally, so to speak; birds do it, bees do it, and so forth. To become one in mind and spirit is a more mysterious thing, and one which requires a more intense, conscious effort.

Paul uses the visible picture of a man and his wife to illustrate the invisible union of Christ to His church.[7] The underlying reality, that a man and his wife unite to form a single spiritual organism of sorts, is used to illustrate that believers united to Christ are like members of a common body. Paul writes about this in many places, famously speaking of believers' distinct spiritual gifts as analogous to different parts of a physical body.[8] He brings this idea back around to plead for believers to strive to become united in mind and spirit.

It's interesting to note in all this that in the church there are gifts which are just given—one is given as an apostle, for example—but there are things which have to be worked for. Paul didn't have to earn the title of apostle; it was given to him. Jesus Himself laid it on him. Paul did have to work out what that meant on a daily basis, and there were responsibilities he carried in that role, but he never stopped being apostolic. When Peter was hypocritical about fellowship with Gentiles and drew down a public rebuke from Paul, Peter never paused being an apostle. He was who he was, and *what* he was.[9]

Being like-minded, though, was something to be pursued. Paul wrote to the church at Philippi, *Therefore if there is any consolation in Christ, if any comfort of love, if any fellowship of the Spirit, if any affection and mercy, fulfill my joy by being like-minded, having the same love, being of one accord, of one mind.*[10]

---

[7] Ephesians 5
[8] 1 Corinthians 12:12-27
[9] Galatians 2:11-21
[10] Philippians 2:1-2

He hoped the find the church there living *"worthy of the gospel of Christ,... that you stand fast in one spirit, with one mind striving together for the faith of the gospel..."*[11]

This is a common concern to Paul; he wrote to Rome, *Now may the God of patience and comfort grant you to be like-minded toward one another, according to Christ Jesus, that you may with one mind* and *one mouth glorify the God and Father of our Lord Jesus Christ.*[12]

To Corinth he wrote, *Now I plead with you, brethren, by the name of our Lord Jesus Christ, that you all speak the same thing, and that there be no divisions among you, but that you be perfectly joined together in the same mind and in the same judgment."*[13] and later on, *Finally, brethren, farewell. Become complete. Be of good comfort, be of one mind, live in peace; and the God of love and peace will be with you.*[14] So many times Paul wrote to address divisions within the church, between Jewish and Gentile believers, between factions and parties or between feuding neighbors, it is no wonder he returns again to this plea.

The apostle Peter shared this concern, writing in his first epistle, *Finally, all of you be of one mind, having compassion for one another; love as brothers, be tenderhearted, be courteous...*[15]

And it was appropriate that Peter and Paul have this unity on their hearts, because Jesus did—and does. *"I do not pray for these alone, but also for those who will believe in Me through their word,"* Jesus prayed before His crucifixion, specifically looking forward to we who believe through the Scriptures

---

[11] Philippians 1:27
[12] Romans 15:5-6
[13] 1 Corinthians 1:10
[14] 2 Corinthians 13:11
[15] 1 Peter 3:8

left by those disciples, *"that they all may be one, as You, Father, are in Me, and I in You; that they also may be one in Us, that the world may believe that You sent Me. And the glory which You gave Me I have given them, that they may be one just as We are one: I in them and You in Me; that they may be made perfect in one, and that the world may know that You have sent Me, and have loved them as You have loved me."*[16]

Believers should be like-minded. When they are, the world begins to see the reality of Christ in our midst and God's love for His people. Jesus' self-sacrificing love for His people and their love for Him are an object lesson for the love between a husband and wife. And when we begin to live up to that high standard, we are holding up a mirror for the world to see—a reflection of the love of Christ. It all works together.

## A Foundation for Unity

It ought to start early. Hal still remembers the advice of a pastor who spoke at his college Bible study on the subject of love and infatuation: "Opposites attract, but 'likes' stay together." We have a fascination with the exotic, but in the long run, it's the commonplace things which draw us along in tandem which keep us united.

The basic principles which guide our lives and our marriage need to be held as common property. If we find ourselves in some disagreement about the basics of life, faith, and relationship, then we need to be talking about them, discussing, perhaps debating them, definitely praying about them until we come to some kind of agreement. Because of the chain of command God has placed in the family, the final responsibility will be the husband's, which means the final decision will have to be his, too. However, his wife and helper needs

---

[16] John 17:20-23

to be *"as iron sharpens iron,"*[17] too. That means that though the final call is the husband's, the wife ought to be sharing her insights and convictions with him—and he should be openly listening and examining his decisions in the light of her wisdom. In that way, we sharpen each other spiritually and grow more together than we ever could apart.

What if you can't come to an agreement, though? What if the husband's final decision is a direct violation of the wife's convictions?

We would say that it depends on how serious the principle really is. If the husband's decision is in *clear* violation of scripture, it's a different situation than a disagreement where real, thinking Christians come down on both sides. If a husband asks his wife to sin, she needs to appeal to his authority, sharing with him lovingly the Word of God, and pray hard he'll change his mind. If he doesn't, she needs to obey the Scripture, in a humble and gentle way. A decision like that should not be done lightly but only when what is asked of the spouse is clearly sinful. Similarly, if a husband finds his wife wants them to engage in sin, he needs to gently and lovingly direct her to the Bible and say no. If she defies him, he is still responsible to do what's right.

Thankfully, those situations are pretty rare. Much more common is the disagreement where both parties have solid Christians on their side. There are a lot of doctrinal and practical differences that believers don't agree on. In these situations, you have a fantastic opportunity to sharpen one another and perhaps bring both of you closer to the truth. How? By reading, listening to discussion, talking it over and praying.

---

[17] Proverbs 27:17

There is no justification for allowing these kinds of differences to divide you—work it out. We once knew a couple who divorced because the wife started attending a church which required ladies to cover their heads. Because her husband didn't agree with this requirement, the wife became convinced that he didn't really know the Lord and left him.

Where do you even start to talk about how wrong that is? However you interpret the passage in question, a person's opinion about women's head scarves is *never* suggested as test of salvation. Even if it were, and her suspicions were well grounded, the wife had no biblical permission for leaving an unbelieving husband. The New Testament clearly tells the Christian spouse to remain with the non-believer as a testimony to them, and not initiate a separation themselves. Better that they had discussed the issue through, and if the husband could not convince his wife to a more charitable view of the subject, perhaps they could have agreed to disagree on this doctrine.

## Converging On A Shared Path

We came to our friendship with differences we knew, and part of the growth of our love for one another came from working through those issues to try and find a common, Biblical ground. As we've turned up unexpected areas where we might have a disagreement, we hash these things out until we come to a place of shared commitment in our principles and convictions. When we stand together on those things, we have so much more unity and peace in our home.

As we become likeminded in principles and convictions, we can really start thinking alike and begin to live our lives together in an intentional and coherent way. Unlike the animals, we don't just respond to life, reacting to different stimuli by instinct. We humans, as the image bearers of God, are living for a purpose, and we should be thinking about what we're doing, examining all things in the light of Scripture. As we walk that path following the convictions we've come to share, we become more and more of one mind.

There are consequences. We discovered that it did absolutely no good for us to split up during a party or event and have separate conversations with the same people. They laughed at us. As we met each person in turn, we found ourselves telling the same story or sharing the same observation as our mate had done, independently, just minutes before. We'd come to think so much alike that if you talked to one of us, you'd talked to both. Now we just stay together at parties—it saves time and embarrassment.

Does that mean we always have the same opinion? No, and if we did, there would hardly be a need for both of us, would there? We do differ on things and discuss ideas, sometimes pretty pointedly, but in general, our response to the outside world is pretty much the same and our disagreements are minor or even trivial. Melanie still hates coffee and peanut butter, and Hal will probably never like broccoli or asparagus. Big deal.

When you use your disagreements as an opportunity to talk over issues and come to a better understanding of one another, discussing and working over the difference to reach a point where you can both stand together, it will tend to make you both more Christ-like. And when you've got someone who is that much in agreement with you, that much on your side, it's a real joy and encouragement!

## ~ 12 ~

## How To Fight So You Both Win

*"Be angry, and do not sin";*
 *do not let the sun go down on your wrath,*
 *nor give place to the devil.*

— Ephesians 4:26-27

We had a formative moment about sundown, standing in a grove of redwood trees on the California coast. And it had nothing to do with the beauty of the evening. It had everything to do with an iron skillet.

In his book *If Only He Knew*, Gary Smalley writes about his interest in couples with successful marriages. He interviewed several of them to ask their secret for long-lasting happiness in relationships. To his surprise, many of them said the same thing: "We go camping."[1]

Camping? The idea puzzled us, too, but when we were newlyweds living on a second lieutenant's pay—about $16,000 our first year together—we didn't have extra money for vacations. If we wanted to see some place distant from family or friends with a guest room, camping was the most affordable way to do it. So "entertainment" aside, that's what we did.

We'd passed our fourth anniversary when we found ourselves newly civilian and newly relocated to sunny (and pricey) California. Our Big Civilian Paycheck purchased less, not more,

[1] Gary T. Smalley, *If Only He Knew* (Grand Rapids, MI: Zondervan, 1997).

than we'd enjoyed on Air Force bases, but the Golden State beckoned. Soon we found ourselves in a state park along the Big Sur highway, happily setting up camp in a cool green grove of redwoods with the setting sun slanting through the treetops, our one-year-old in his playpen beside the tent, our new Coleman stove open for business.

And the fateful moment came.

Hal turned to Melanie and said, "Where's the frying pan?"

And she looked back with a innocent puzzlement and said, "I thought *you* packed it."

Cue the dramatic music.

It suddenly dawned on us that we had come away to the wilderness with everything we needed except something to cook in. No pan, no griddle, no pot, *nothing*. We had hot dogs and chili for supper, eggs and toast for the morning, but no spatula to turn them with and nothing to turn them *in*. And it was hours to the nearest town.

Hal felt a rise of irritation. He thought *she* had packed it. Wasn't she the manager of the kitchen? He packed the tent and sleeping bags and other gear; she took care of the womanly part, right?

Melanie was annoyed, too. She'd loaded the dishpan with all the heavy cooking supplies and was sure she'd asked Hal to carry it out. And here we stood.

At that moment, a thought dawned on him.

*Here we have a wonderful opportunity to hold an excellent, clear cut argument,* he thought. *I thought she had it, she really should have, and I'm perfectly just to point that out to her.*

*On the other hand,* he thought, *that won't get me supper.*

*So what do I want—a slam dunk win against my wife? Or something to eat? Because win, lose, or draw, all the argument in the world isn't going to get us fed.*

On later reflection, Hal admitted that either one of them could have gotten that pan, and either of them could have checked to make sure they had it before they left. Certainly Melanie wasn't the only responsible adult in the family.

Melanie remembers a very similar moment standing at the end of the picnic table, wanting to lash out, wanting to blow up. She remembers it as clearly as if it were yesterday, though it's over twenty years ago. Sarcastic remarks started welling up in her mind and she began to justify them to herself.

*He knows very well he should have carried that heavy thing out. I can't believe this! I feel like screaming at him. It's all his fault.*

*What then, though?* Her thoughts continued. *We have a big fight, say awful things we'll just have to repent of, and poor little John still has nothing to eat and we've scared him to death, to boot.*

And what actually happened is part of the history. We both decided it was better to fix supper than fix blame. The issue then became how to adapt to the situation. Golfers understand you have to play the ball where it lies. It's a useful concept for much of life, we've found. We had a situation—lack of a pan—that required a solution.

We decided to cook the hot dogs directly on the grill of the camp stove—a little extra cleaning would be needed, but it would do the trick. And we could probably heat the chili directly in the can, which we did (take the lid off first, we note). After supper, we carefully washed out the can and saved it up for breakfast, when it became an awkward but serviceable way to cook scrambled eggs. And stacking the bread around the edges of the stove against the lid got it warm and kind of toast-like.

Frankly, we don't remember how we managed the other meals. The important lesson, though, was that the argument we nearly had would not have fixed the situation one bit. Both the victor and the vanquished would end up staring at each other across a darkening pinic table as night fell on a world still without supper. This is what's known as a Pyrrhic victory. And it's a win that's not worth the cost.

Since then, we found there are ways not only to disagree without being disagreeable, as many people urge, but to find real victory in an apparent defeat. As in the conflict of nations, couples often achieve more when they seem to retreat.

## It's Inevitable

We heard the story of a couple so beautifully matched and so amazingly compatible, they were never known to quarrel. Peace and harmony ruled their little cottage for nearly fifty years. Then one day, it happened—a cross word was said, tears flowed, repentence followed. The elderly husband looked down at the little woman in his arms and said, "Dear, let's not fight until the honeymoon is over."

We appreciate the spirit of the story, but that's just not real life. Dave Harvey grabbed the best book title when he published *When Sinners Say 'I Do.'* One student comes home from college and tells his high school friends, "Well, I found the perfect girl." "Did you go out with her?" they asked. "No," he shrugs, "she was looking for the perfect man."

The rest of us make do with the lovable but fallen sinners we know—sinners just like ourselves. The fruit of living in a broken world with a damaged soul is the truth that eventually, sooner rather than later, we will be frustrated, disappointed, hurt in some way. That prompts us to irritability, or to push back, lash out, seek to retaliate.

*Where do wars and fights* come *from among you?* asked the apostle James.

> *Do they not come from your desires for pleasure that war in your members? You lust and do not have. You murder and covet and cannot obtain. You fight and war. Yet you do not have because you do not ask. You ask and do not receive, because you ask amiss, that you may spend it on your pleasures.*[2]

Murder is mixed in there and shouldn't be glossed over. Most relationships don't get so fractured that blood is split, yet there are different kinds of murder in the Bible. Cain resented the favor God showed toward his brother Abel, and though God cautioned him and showed Cain a better way, he brooded himself into a rage and struck his brother down.[3] That's clearly going too far, yet there is a more insidious offense.

If an ordinary man had preached the Sermon on the Mount, we'd say it was a brilliant piece of spiritual teaching. Coming from the lips of Jesus Himself, it is a binding pronouncement.

---

[2] James 4:1-3
[3] Genesis 4:1-8

He warns that the sin of lust incurs God's wrath the same as the consummated act of adultery, and He warns that an unjust anger with a brother carries the spiritual harm of murder:

> *"You have heard that it was said to those of old, 'You shall not murder, and whoever murders will be in danger of the judgment.' But I say to you that whoever is angry with his brother without a cause shall be in danger of the judgment. And whoever says to his brother, 'Raca!' shall be in danger of the council. But whoever says, 'You fool!' shall be in danger of hell fire."*[4]

The word Jesus uses for judgment is the same for cases of anger as for murder, and it is the term used for the final reckoning of God against all sins—*it is appointed for men to die once, but after this the judgment.*[5]

In case you missed it in the Gospels, the apostle John also wrote in his pastoral correspondence that *Whoever hates his brother is a murderer.*[6] So we can't take any comfort in the fact that we've avoided slaughter thus far. Unrighteous anger is a serious sin.

## A Time for Conflict

It probably should be mentioned that there is a time for conflict or even anger in relationships. When Job was bereaved of his children, robbed of his belongings, and broken in health, his wife said to him, *"Do you still hold fast to your integrity? Curse God and die!"* (What encouraging counsel, dear!)

---

[4] Matthew 5:21-22
[5] Hebrews 9:27
[6] 1 John 3:15 (ESV)

*But he said to her, "You speak as one of the foolish
women speaks. Shall we indeed accept good from
God, and shall we not accept adversity?" In all this
Job did not sin with his lips.*[7]

When Abigail rushed to supply to David's request for pro-
visions—thereby heading off a retaliatory action against her
arrogant husband's entire tribe—she frankly admitted to David
that her husband Nabal (his name means literally, "Fool") was
a "worthless fellow." The narrative introduces him as *"harsh
and evil in* his *doings,"* and Abigail pleads David's mercy toward
them all, saying *"Please, let not my lord regard this scoundrel
Nabal. For as his name* is, *so is he:... folly* is *with him!"* If not
anger, there is at least a note of desperation in her words, a
recognition that if left to himself, the pride of her husband
could be the death or impoverishment of them all.[8]

In both situations, faithful spouses found themselves at
odds with mates who were clearly opposing God's will. When
the honor and reputation of God and Christ are at stake,
sometimes you have to take a stand for the truth. Even the
apostles had their moments. When Peter began to compromise the Gospel out of fear of the Jews in Antioch, Paul says
*"I withstood him to his face, because he was to be blamed"* in
his hypocrisy.[9] Job's wife advised blasphemy, Nabal sneered
at God's anointed choice for king, Peter began to backslide
from grace into legalism. They *deserved* rebuke.

As Christians, too, we need to be honest enough to admit
that often we fall short of what we hope to be, and when
a rebuke comes our way, we should be ready to consider
it. The Proverbs suggest that a loving challenge can be like

---

[7] Job 2:9-10
[8] 1 Samuel 25:2-35
[9] Galatians 2:11-14

iron sharpening iron—throwing sparks perhaps and abrading rough edges, even causing discomfort for a time, but with the ultimate end of improving one another.[10]

There are a couple of ways we can approach criticism. One is what we might call the "Balaam's Ass" approach. In one of the most remarkable accounts in Scripture, the prophet Balaam was bribed by King Balak of Moab to curse the people of Israel as they moved toward Jericho. On his errand, Balaam was surprised to find his donkey balking, crushing him against a stone wall, and eventually lying down in the middle of the pathway. When he beat the infuriating animal, Balaam was verbally rebuked *by the offended donkey*—and the Lord revealed that the animal had actually prevented the Angel of the Lord from striking Balaam.[11]

The point? Sometimes you'll get good advice or criticism, even rebuke, from someone you'd rather not hear it from. Balaam was so angry with his donkey he didn't seem to notice *the animal* was speaking to him. Yet the donkey's stubbornness which so displeased the faithless prophet was a lifesaver. We need to be open to receiving counsel from any source which God chooses—the point is not whether we're eager to be taught by our farm animal, an irritating co-worker, or even our spouse, but whether their advice might be wisdom from heaven.

When Jesus gathered his disciples for their last Passover together, He announced that one of their number would betray Him. *And they were exceeding sorrowful, and each of them began to say to Him, "Lord, is it I?"*[12] That is a much better response to criticism; each of the disciples but one considered the re-

---

[10] Proverbs 27:6, 17
[11] Numbers 22:1-35
[12] Matthew 26:22 (NKJV)

buke and asked himself first, "Could I be at fault here?" even when they knew they had no intention to do such a thing. They loved the Lord and were not offended but saddened to think they might cause Him offense. Even though our spouse has his or her shortcomings, wouldn't it make for peace if our first response to criticism was to consider our failings with humility rather than defend them with pride?

Honestly, most of our disagreements are not grand drama, like Martin Luther confronting the Emperor's demand to retract his teaching—"Here I stand, I can do no other. God help me!"[13] Dramatic moments are riveting precisely because they are rare. Real life is more often about who left the cap off the toothpaste or who forgot to put the gas bill in the mailbox.

So if conflict is a fact of real life in marriage, it makes sense to think about how to deal with it.

God gave Moses directions how the Israelites were to settle their differences. *"You shall not hate your brother in your heart,"* God told him,

> *"You shall surely rebuke your neighbor, and not bear sin because of him. You shall not take vengeance, nor bear any grudge against the children of your people, but you shall love your neighbor as yourself..."*[14]

---

[13] If you're not caught up on your church history, in 1521 Martin Luther was summoned before the Holy Roman Emperor Charles V and representatives of Pope Leo X who challenged him to recant his Biblical teachings. After a night of fervent prayer, in the face of excommunication and possible torture, Luther was said to sum up his refusal with those words.

[14] Leviticus 19:17-18

If God expects this kind of consideration between neighbors, people no closer than those attending the same church with you or sharing a property line at home, surely He means at least as much between two-made-one-flesh.

Before we engage each other in controversy, it's worth considering one possibility—simply letting the other person have their way. When the church in Corinth was full of divisions and arguments, the apostle Paul rebuked them for dragging one another into the civil courts. *[It] is already an utter failure for you that you go to law against one another,* he wrote. *Why do you not rather accept wrong? Why do you not rather let yourselves be cheated?*[15]

What, just roll over and take it? Let your spouse *win?*

Well, *yes,* that seems to be what Paul is saying. Maybe out of love for your spouse and a desire to avoid conflict, you can give up your right to the argument. Paul writes in another place that we should be *kindly affectionate to one another... in honor giving preference to one another.*[16] To the church in Philippi he urged, *in lowliness of mind let each esteem others better than himself.*[17] Some things are truly not worth arguing over, and when we can recognize these and graciously submit to one another, often conflict will be avoided completely.

The important point though is to recognize when you really can't let it go, whether for matters of high principle or simply knowing you can't be gracious enough to give in and not resent it. When God told the Israelites not to harbor a grudge, He intended for them to work toward peace with each other.

---

[15] 1 Corinthians 6:7
[16] Romans 12:10
[17] Philippians 2:3

## Don't Let Hatred Take Root

An elder professor at a Christian college used to say, "The heart of the problem is the problem of the heart." God warned Moses that hatred in the heart—even if it's never expressed—leads to sin for the hater. Paul said, many centuries later, *Be angry and do not sin; do not let the sun go down on your wrath.*[18]

That, by the way, was one of the early principles of our marriage. If we ever had a disagreement, we wouldn't go to bed mad; we stayed up as long as it took to work it out. We've had some late bedtimes because of it, but it has really helped us establish a habit of getting over an argument. After all this time, neither of us has the heart to stay angry with the other.

Dealing with our conflicts each day meant never allowing opportunities to nurse grudges or build up resentment. Bitterness takes time and unresolved anger to grow. Purposing to deal with it right away, even when it isn't at all convenient, means we foresee trouble coming and hide ourselves—it's just prudent.[19]

Just like Paul was compelled to oppose Peter when truth was at stake, there will be times to stand on principle—but more frequently, times to clear the air because of our own weakness. As Ecclesiastes says, there is a season and a time for every purpose under heaven.[20] While we should turn the other cheek whenever we can, as Jesus taught us, we shouldn't let matters sit and fester. If something in our marriage is so

---

[18] Ephesians 4:26
[19] Proverbs 22:3
[20] Ecclesiastes 3:1-8

eating at us that we find resentment and even hatred taking root, we need to address that temptation for what it is.

The ticklish thing is to engage disagreements with respect, with gentleness even.

## To fight right, you have to follow the rules

Any soldier knows that when a conflict breaks out, there are rules of engagement. Even warfare has something of civilization and ethics behind it, and certain types of conduct are simply out of bounds for the ethical soldier. We realized the same is true if disputes arise between the nation of Hal and the nation of Melanie.

When God says to "reason frankly" (other translations say "reprove" or "rebuke"), He uses a word common to legal cases. There's a sense of restraint and decorum, of respect even when it's plain—to one party, at least—that the other person is in the wrong. God desires us to work out our differences by coming to understanding, not by overwhelming the other with physical or verbal force.

## Rule 1: No Nuclear Option

After World War II, an uneasy truce existed between the United States and the Soviet Union. It stood on a doctrine we called Mutually Assured Destruction. Each nation had the ability to destroy the other, and we both had the ability to see the blow coming. If you launch your missiles against me, I'll launch mine in response, and we will totally destroy both nations within the hour.

We were so dependent on this balanced threat, the idea of a defensive shield which could stop incoming missiles in flight was considered destabilizing. Anything which gave one side the ability to survive a nuclear strike removed the security of the other. It was pretty sick.

What is the most destructive response to conflict in a marriage—short of bloodshed? It's the murder of the relationship, the death of the union by divorce. God allows it in certain cases, but He hates it all the same.[21]

We have a dear friend who was divorced before she became a believer, and she is now remarried to another Christian. Every time they have a serious argument, she considers leaving him. Sometimes in the heat of the moment they suggest it to one another.

Occasionally she calls, sure that this time, it's really over. The conversation follows a familiar path.

"So what Biblical grounds do you have for divorce?" Melanie asks her. "Has he committed adultery?"

No, never.

"Abandonment? Rejecting the faith?"

Well, no.

"Oh," Melanie concludes. "Well, if you want to do right, then you guys have no choice but to get over it." They always do, but raising the specter of separation and divorce is damaging to their relationship, and it disturbs the children who overhear them.

---

[21] Micah 2:14-15

What if we agree together that we meant it when we said our marriage vows "until death do us part"—the actual demise of one or the other? What if we said that, come what may, we would not consider the final Doomsday scenario for our one flesh? What if we decide we won't exercise the nuclear option against our spouse—not even in self defense?

It makes a whale of a difference in the time of marital conflict, if you have already committed yourselves to staying on board. If you both agree that come what may, you're in this boat for the full journey, it increases your chances of working through the difficult parts of the river. While we were engaged, we agreed that ending the marriage would never be an option. Knowing that we'd be looking at each other over breakfast for the rest of our lives was a great encouragement to go ahead and work things out as we went along. Really, was any argument so bad that we expected to stay mad for forty or fifty years more? Then why wait decades to settle it?

Taking the nuclear option completely off the table means that when conflict arises, you are going to have to work it out. That realization gives you the motivation to fight fair, to get it over with, to get through it.

**No cluster bombs.** Everyone's seen film of nuclear warheads detonating. Another shockingly effective weapon is the cluster bomb, a conventional munition which dispenses dozens or hundreds of small bomblets over a wide area. The effect is like a hailstorm of hand grenades, and it can be devastating against certain softer targets like troop formations, supply depots, and vehicle concentrations.

You and your spouse are like troops in exposed positions. If you need to engage a particular problem or deal with a particular threat, it is destructive to attack targets on all sides at once. Better to aim at the specific thing which needs to change now, than to hurl charges at old mistakes and unrelated issues, opening old wounds and causing new ones.

In other words, decide what you're going to address, and don't keep throwing the kitchen sink at the culprit. Have one argument at a time, and only for good and sufficient reasons— the kind you are ready to explain at God's judgment seat.

**No assassinations.** Sometimes one of our children comes in angry and crying. What's wrong, we ask, and with a huff and harumph, they blurt out a sibling's name. No, we tell them, your *brother* is not the problem; something your brother *said* or *did* is the problem. We try to get them to focus on problem *behaviors*, not problem *people*. Your spouse is not the problem, but something they did or keep on doing is the issue you want to address.

Major character issues and infuriating habits take time to correct; don't make a character case out of a single incident this day.

**When the conflict is over, make sure it's over.** Sometimes in the course of a disagreement, armies will agree to a cease-fire for a time; unless they reach a negotiated agreement during that period, though, it's just a temporary calm with a sense of impending sense of unfinished business. The First World War ended with an armistice, and a generation later resumed business under new management. The Korean peninsula has been in a state of alarm and tension since the mid-1950s. The first Gulf War led to a second.

When a matter is truly dealt with, though, it should be honorably and charitably concluded. When we forgive our mates, it should be true forgiveness.

Real forgiveness is an ongoing act where we look the offender in the face and say, "I now consider this matter forgiven and I will not bring it up again. All is well." It's not choosing to ignore or simply forgetting the offense, but choosing no longer to hold the offender responsible for it.

God of course is our example. When He made a new convenant with His people, He said, *"I will forgive their iniquity, and their sin I will remember no more."*[22] Does God still know that His people had sinned against Him? Absolutely, in every detail. But there are memories which stand out in our minds' eye, unbidden, and then there is the act of calling them back to mind, of rehearsing the matter and holding someone to account for it—*actively* remembering. When God forgives, He doesn't lose His knowledge of the wrong, but He stamps it "PAID" for the sake of Jesus' suffering.[23] He doesn't pull it out of a heavenly file cabinet and shake it in our faces, thundering, "There you go again, like you always do! I've about had it with you!" When it's forgiven, it's been dealt with, and it's not supposed to come back. When God removes our transgressions from us *"As far as the east is from the west,"*[24] He doesn't send them orbiting around the globe to hit us again from behind. They're *gone.*

So when we settle our differences and forgiveness is granted, that is the last time we allow ourselves to dwell on the

---

[22] Jeremiah 31:34

[23] In fact, when Jesus gave up His spirit and died on the cross, his last word was "It is finished!"—in New Testament Greek, the single word, *"Tetelestai!"* It's a commercial word which was used to indicate payment of a debt or completion of some other duty or obligation.

[24] Psalm 103:12

offense. We don't keep score against each other. That means we can't use the time-honored complaints "You always..." or "You did it again..." or "That's just like you..." If an offense is forgiven, it shouldn't be brought up again. There should be no double jeopardy in our family.

## It *Is* Possible to Both Win

When Hal was in the paper industry, one of the mills where he worked went through a contract negotiation with the union. This particular mill and the locals which organized it had a fairly peaceable relationship, with just a bit of tension which was probably healthy accountability on both sides. As the old contract drew to a close, the company brought in a consultant who met with leaders on both sides of the table and presented the concept of win-win negotiation—basically, that if both sides were respectful of one another, honest about their needs, and willing to try and find good faith solutions which would benefit both the company and the workers, it was truly possible for both management and labor to emerge with an acceptable contract.

If that works in an adversarial industrial context—and it did—then certainly we who are one flesh with one another, submitted to the same Lord, and guided by the same Holy Spirit—when we're willing to listen to Him—should expect the same outcome.

Though we may have never seen a "fair fight" between husband and wife, perhaps watching our parents blow up and walk out, or give one another a chilly reception for days or *months* rather than resolve an issue, that sort of mutual win should be our goal. *If it is possible, as much as depends on you, live peaceably with all men,* wrote Paul.[25] "*Blessed are the*

25 Romans 12:18

peacemakers," said Jesus, "*for they shall be called the children of God.*"[26] The apostle James wrote that *the wisdom that is from above is first pure, then peaceable, gentle, willing to yield, full of mercy and good fruits...*[27] Tone down the accusatory tone, don't call names, constantly reassure each other of our love and respect, and always work for reconciliation.

And when the time comes to forgive and move on, do it like God does—freely, completely, and without fear. What a tremendous, liberating thing that can be!

---

[26] Matthew 5:9
[27] James 3:17

# Conclusion

*My beloved spoke, and said to me,*
*"Rise up, my love, my fair one,*
*And come away.*
*For lo, the winter is past,*
*The rain is over and gone."*

— Song of Solomon 2:10-11

Power and its pursuit can be overwhelming to a man, and the relentless ambition which drives a man up the ladder of his career has often left a trail of broken marriages and shattered relationships in its wake.

The pursuit to become a member of the most exclusive fraternity in America, the Presidency, is no exception and may be worse than most. Many of the First Ladies disappear into the mists of history, and their personal stories are seldom told. Many of them are studies of betrayal and loneliness. We may remember scenes of Hillary Clinton standing tight-lipped beside her husband as his dalliance with a young White House intern was investigated and debated on camera for interminable months. Stories of JFK's extramarital adventures have circulated for five decades since his death. Some of the worst of FDR's infidelity didn't reach the news until the 1960's, but his multiple affairs so fractured the relationship that Eleanor moved out and at one time, even refused to return to him when he was seriously ill. The White House takes a toll on its occupants, and often their home life.

But then you have John and Abigail Adams.

If colleagues were asked one word to describe John Adams, it would have been "ambitious." He stepped in to defend the British soldiers accused of the Boston Massacre. He sailed for Europe under the nose of the Royal Navy to try and negotiate war loans from the Dutch. He endured volumes of personal political abuse in the muckraking media. It was all part of being a public servant—and done with an eye on the possibility of advancement.

But biographer David McCollough notes early on that "His marriage to Abigail Smith was the most important decision of John Adams's life, as would become apparent with time. She was in all respects his equal and the part she was to play would be greater than he could possibly have imagined, for all his love for her and what appreciation he already had of her beneficial, steadying influence."[1]

When he courted her as a young attorney, his letters were addressed to "Ever Dear Diana," the Roman goddess of the moon, or "Miss Adorable." Hers in return usually began, "My Dearest Friend"—a salutation she used for decades to come. In one of the only times Adams opens his diary in those hectic years, he wrote:

> *Di was a constant feast. Tender, feeling, sensible, friendly. A friend. Not an imprudent, not an indelicate, not a disagreeable word of action. Prudent, soft, sensible, obliging, active.*

"She saw what latent abilities and strengths were in her ardent suitor and was deeply in love," McCollough writes.

---

1 David McCollough, *John Adams* (New York: Simon & Schuster, 2001), p. 57.

"Where others might see a stout, bluff little man, she saw a giant of great heart, and so it was ever to be."[2]

The language of lovers did not end with the wedding. Years later, as President Adams stood on the top rung of the political ladder, he would write desperately when his wife was away:

> "I must go to you or you must come to me. I cannot live without you," he wrote. And again: "I must entreat you to lose not a moment's time in preparing to come on, that you may take off from me every care of life but that of my public duty, assist me with your councils, and console me with your conversation."

> "The times are crucial and dangerous, and I must have you here to assist me," he told her. "I must now repeat this with zeal and earnestness. I can do nothing without you."[3]

Years of dangerous diplomatic work during the war required John to be abroad while Abigail kept the home and children in Massachusetts. The separation was hard on both of them, McCollough wrote, but "[she] would have him no other way than he was; she wished no other for him; she wanted him to be where he was doing his utmost for the country. And still she desperately wanted him with her."[4]

As she lay dying of typhoid at the age of 74, John came down from her bedside and said, "in an energetic voice, 'I wish I could lie down beside her and die, too.'"[5] Their son John Quincy, who traveled with his father during the war

2 McCollough, p. 53.
3 McCollough, p. 479.
4 McCollough, p. 144.
5 McCollough, p. 623.

and began his government career at the age of 14, was inaugurated as president shortly after Abigail's death. "For years afterward, whenever complimented about John Quincy and his role in national life, and the part he had played as father, Adams would say with emphasis, 'My son had a mother!'"[6]

And as he observed to his diary a generation before, and as she had written in her love notes and her everyday correspondence, John and Abigail had a friendship. It was a love affair, a political union, an arrangement of comfort and support and mutual challenge. Even in an era when formality and a certain coldness was considered correct behavior, and when the roles of men and women were much more restricted that they are today, John and Abigail were open, free, transparent, and passionate toward one another—whether the subject was their mutual love, or national politics, or the progress of their retirement farm "Peace Field."

The story of John and Abigail should challenge and encourage us in the same way. They endured the stress of war, uncertain economies, job insecurity, public attack, long separation, and the death of children. Nevertheless, they began as friends. They continued to share interests; they communicated frequently; they endured struggles with each other's help; they looked to God as the source of their strength, provision, and guidance. And they never, never lost their vision of their lover as their best friend.

If the Adamses could go through all the trials they did and still remain fast friends, then why don't we?

When God created marriage, the very first thing He said about it was *It is not good that man should be alone.* Before He talked about shared mission, the joy of sex, or the dominion

---

6 McCollough, p. 626.

mandate, He talked about companionship. It will not be our first thought every moment, and it will not be the most urgent facet of our relationship each hour, but it has the pride of first mention, and it will give you support and comfort in the midst of troubles and serve as an amplifier for your joys.

We hope we've been able to encourage you to see your spouse in a new, more Biblical way. We hope that you will be able to join the lovers in Solomon's song who look to one another and say, now and forever,

*This is my beloved, and this is my friend.*

# Colophon

This book is set in Fontin, a modern font family chosen for its clarity and sensible tone, while also imparting a subtle grace. Designed by Jos Buivenga and released by his foundry Exljbris, the original serif Fontin is accompanied by an excellent sans-serif. Its airy tone and classical lines complement the text well as the display face.

Cover design and layout by Hal Young. Cover photography by Nicolas Machard and John Calvin Young. Interior layout, design, and typesetting by John Calvin Young.